12 MONTHS OF FUN!

THE LOBSTER KIDS' GUIDE
TO EXPLORING
CHICAGO

BY ED AVIS

Lobster Press™

Avis, Ed, 1967-
The Lobster Kids' Guide to Exploring Chicago: 12 Months of Fun!
Text copyright © 2001 Lobster Press™
Illustrations copyright © 2001 Lobster Press™

Published by Lobster Press™
1620 Sherbrooke St. W., Suites C & D
Montréal, Québec H3H 1C9
Tel. (514) 904-1100, Fax (514) 904-1101
www.lobsterpress.com

Publisher: Alison Fripp
Editor: Bob Kirner
Assistant Editor: Alison Fischer
Copy Editor: Frances Purslow
Cover and Illustrations: Christine Battuz
Icons: Christiane Beauregard and Josée Masse
Layout and Design: Olivier Lasser

Distribution:

In the United States
Advanced Global
Distribution Services
5880 Oberlin Drive, Suite 400
San Diego, CA 92121
Tel. (858) 457-2500
Fax (858) 812-6476

In Canada
Raincoast Books
9050 Shaughnessey Street
Vancouver, BC V6P 6E5
Tel. 1-800-663-5714
Fax 1-800-565-3770

We acknowledge the financial support of the Government of Canada through the Book Publishing Industry Development Program (BPIDP) for our publishing activities.

This guidebook makes reference to various trademarks, marks and characters owned by Disney Enterprises, Inc. and are used by permission from Disney Enterprises, Inc.

National Library of Canada Cataloguing in Publication Data

Avis, Ed, 1967-
    The Lobster kids' guide to exploring chicago: 12 months of fun!

Includes Index.
ISBN 1-894222-40-7

    1. Family recreation—Illinois—Chicago—Guidebooks.
2. Children—Travel—Illinois—Chicago—Guidebooks.
3. Amusements—Illinois—Chicago—Guidebooks.
4. Chicago (Ill.)—Guidebooks. I. Battuz, Christine II. Kirner, Bob, 1959—
III. Title

F548.18.A95 2001   917.73'11044   C2001-900034-0

Printed and bound in Canada

Table of Contents

Author's Introduction

I f you live in the Chicago area or you are visiting, consider yourself lucky because it's a community that puts warmth ahead of speed and friendliness ahead of business. Spending time in the windy city is the ideal way to introduce your children to urban living—diverse cultures, stimulating activities, unparalleled educational opportunities and great food!

Chicago is overflowing with thousands of kid-friendly activities, from parks to museums to children's theatre. This guide will provide you with great ideas for a wide variety of exciting outings. Whether you live in the area or are just passing through, be prepared to learn, explore and play all day.

This book is dedicated to two special young people who helped make it happen, my sons Nathan and Benjamin. They gamely trekked off with daddy on scores of "adventures," usually in our trusty red jogging stroller. From the top of the Sears Tower to the marsh at North Park Village Nature Center, Nate and Ben explored and played and probed, always making sure I saw things from their point of view. We tackled this great city together and we are infinitely richer for it.

ED AVIS

A Word from the Publisher

L obster Press™ published its first book, *The Lobster Kids' Guide to Exploring Montréal*, in 1998. Since then, the Kids' City Explorer Series has grown and now includes guides to other major Canadian cities. Due to the resounding success of the Canadian series, this year Lobster Press™ is publishing books for families exploring cities in the United States.

Whether you're a tourist, resident, parent or teacher, this book is a complete resource of things to do and see with kids in the Chicago area. It's jam-packed with valuable, timesaving information and great ideas for outings.

Ed Avis and his sons visited the sites in this guide in 2000-2001. All information provided has been verified. However, since prices and business hours are subject to change, call ahead to avoid disappointment. Please accept our apologies in advance for any inconveniences you may encounter.

To get the most out of this guide, please familiarize yourself with our "Lobster Rating System" and table of icons. These features let you know what Ed's family thought of each site and what amenities are available. Please note that traveling distances to the sites were determined from Grant Park.

If you have comments about this book, visit our website and complete our on-line survey. Let us know if we've missed your family's favorite destination, and we'll include it in the next edition!

One last word: Please be careful when you and your children visit the sites from the guide. Neither Lobster Press™ nor the author can be held responsible for any accidents that might occur.

Enjoy! And watch for the other books in the Kids' City Explorer Series. Now available: Boston, Las Vegas, San Francisco and Seattle. Coming in 2002: Halifax, Miami, New Orleans, Quebec City and San Diego.

FROM THE GANG AT LOBSTER PRESS™

The Lobster Rating System

We thought it would be helpful if you knew what Ed Avis and his family thought about the sites in this book before you head off to visit them. They rated every attraction and activity they visited for its:

☞ enjoyment level for children
☞ learning opportunities for children
☞ accessibility from the Grant Park
☞ costs and value for the money

A one-lobster rating: Good attraction.

A two-lobster rating: Very good attraction.

A three-lobster rating: Excellent attraction.

Not fitting some of the criteria, and subsequently not rated, are green spaces and various similar, nearby or other attractions.

Table of Icons

These facilities and/or activities are represented by the following icons:

Bicycling		Parking	
Birthday parties		Picnic tables	
Bus stop		Playground	
Coat check		Restaurant/ snack bar	
First aid		Restroom	
Hiking		Skating	
Ice cream stand		Swimming	
In-line skating		Telephone	
Information centre		Wheelchair/stroller accessible	
El Stop		Wildlife watching	

CHAPTER 1

LOCAL
ATTRACTIONS

Introduction

C hicago is considered one of the most livable large cities in America; residents and regular visitors know why. Vibrant, exciting and packed with things to do, Chicago is a kid-friendly town that's clean and easy to navigate.

You can start your family's Windy City adventure by taking in the awesome view of the city from atop the John Hancock Center, then spend the rest of the morning shopping the Magnificent Mile. If it's peaceful surroundings you're after, head to the Chicago River Walk to watch the boats and ducks. There's no end to the way kids can express themselves creatively at the Kraft Education Center in the Art Institute of Chicago. If you prefer your art outside, take a walking tour and view the sculptures in the Loop. Kids love sliding down the Picasso work in the Daley Center Plaza.

Fun's the name of the game at Navy Pier with its giant Ferris wheel and boat rides. The Chicago Children's Museum, also on the pier, has three floors of engaging displays that promise hands-on fun and learning. When it's mealtime, you'll find an elaborate food court and sit-down restaurants for lunching on the pier. Then get ready for more exploring along the lakefront path, Grant Park or at the Field Museum.

One thing is guaranteed: whatever sites you decide to see, at the end of the day your kids will head home tired and happy.

Art in the City
THE ART INSTITUTE
OF CHICAGO

III S. Michigan Ave., Chicago
(312) 443-3600
www.artic.edu

T he Art Institute is a world-class museum with a kid-sensitive side. The fun tour begins in the Kraft Education Center on the lower level (take the staircase or elevator behind the counter at the Michigan Avenue entrance). Young kids enjoy playing with the blocks and educational toys in the Family Room. Across from it, the Kids' Exhibition is designed to stimulate artistic thought through play and observation. Older children like visiting the Thorne Miniature Rooms gallery. Its tiny model rooms representing European and American historic homes can be examined up close.

At certain times of the week, kids can create their own art in the Artist's Studio. The art themes are tied to the main exhibition and professional artists work with the children (reservations not required). Your visit to the Kraft Education Center should include a tour of the offbeat photo exhibit too.

Don't overlook the "grownup" exhibits in the Art Institute proper. The collection, which encompasses everything from famous Impressionist paintings to ancient African sculpture, has turned many kids on to art. One of the most popular exhibits, the George

F. Harding Collection of Arms and Armor, contains hundreds of swords, daggers, coats of armor and other items seemingly straight out of the land of knights and fairy-tale castles.

SEASONS AND TIMES
➤ Year-round: Mon—Fri, 10:30 am—4:30 pm (Tue until 8 pm); Sat—Sun, 10 am—5 pm. Closed Thanksgiving and Christmas.

COST
➤ Adults $8, seniors and students $5, under 6 free. Free on Tuesdays. Certain exhibitions require special tickets. Annual memberships available.

GETTING THERE
➤ The Art Institute sits at the north end of Grant Park on Michigan Ave. You can park in the Monroe St. underground public pay parking garage at the corner of Monroe and Michigan, or in any of the pay lots west of Michigan.
➤ By public transit, take any of the El lines that circle the Loop to Adams St. and walk east on Adams to the museum. Or take any of the CTA buses that run along Michigan.

NEARBY
➤ Chicago Cultural Center, Grant Park, the lakefront, Chicago River.

COMMENT
➤ The Court Cafeteria is an inexpensive place for lunch. Plan a 2-hour visit.

Fun for All Ages
CHICAGO CHILDREN'S MUSEUM

700 E. Grand Ave. (on Navy Pier), Chicago
(312) 527-1000
www.chichildrensmuseum.org

The Chicago Children's Museum features three floors of engaging educational displays that stimulate kids' minds and burn up energy. Treehouse Trails is a popular spot for younger children. They can climb through a wooden tree fort and push buttons to hear bird sounds, catch fish from a rowboat and dress up in animal costumes. Older kids can't wait to get to WaterWays, where they can construct fountains out of pipe and valves, direct the flow of a river through plastic dams and stretch their muscles on a series of human-powered pumps. Teens will find mental stimulation in the Inventing Lab building all kinds of contraptions, including a glider that works.

Hours of hands-on fun await kids at the museum's other exhibits. Safe and Sound has an ambulance, a doctor's office and a half dozen other stations displaying health and safety basics. Under Construction has real tools and building supplies, while Playmaze features a mock school bus, a car wash and a grocery store where little ones can play make-believe. Save time for the Dinosaur Expedition and the Kovler Family Climbing Schooner.

Temporary exhibits liven up the museum for regular visitors and its location on Navy Pier (page 30) ensures you'll find plenty to do after your visit.

SEASONS AND TIMES
➤ Summer (Memorial Day—Labor Day): Daily, 10 am—5 pm (Thu until 8 pm). Winter: Summer hours but closed Mondays.

COST
➤ Adults and children $6.50, seniors $5.50, under 1 free. Free on Thursdays after 5 pm. Memberships available.

GETTING THERE
➤ By car, take Lake Shore Dr. north to the Illinois Ave. Exit. Go east on Illinois and follow the signs to Navy Pier. Pay parking available in garages on the pier. About 10 minutes from Grant Park.
➤ By public transit, take CTA bus 29 (State St.) or 65 (Grand Ave.) to the pier's front entrance. A free trolley travels between Navy Pier and State. Board it beside the "Navy Pier Trolley Stop" sign.
➤ By bicycle, take the lakefront path directly to Navy Pier.

NEARBY
➤ Other Navy Pier attractions (includes the Ferris wheel and carousel), Ohio St. Beach.

COMMENT
➤ The first-floor gift shop offers a variety of educational toys. Kids won't want to leave this museum. Plan at least a 2-hour visit.

Down by the River
CHICAGO RIVER WALK

**East Branch of the Chicago River (between street
numbers 300 and 400 N.), Chicago**

N ow rejuvenated, the Chicago River is a
defining characteristic of the city and an ideal
place for biking, in-line skating or simply
going out for a walk. A concrete pathway follows the
river on and off throughout the Loop and is often
within a few feet of the water. Along the way, kids can
wave to the people on the boats, gondolas and water
bikes and peer at the enormous steel bridges that
span the river overhead. Small restaurants with tables
beside the water are pleasant spots for lunching.

For most of the way through the Loop, the path
exists only between the bridges. Once you reach a
bridge, you will have to climb the steps, cross the
street and then descend another set of steps to re-
sume your tour. A nicely landscaped stretch on the
south bank of the river extends from Michigan
Avenue to Lake Michigan and is highlighted by a
well-lit tunnel under Lake Shore Drive. At the far
end of the tunnel, the path runs south for about 50
feet, then splits. Continue south and you'll end up
in Grant Park (page 23); go north and you'll cross
the river on lower Lake Shore Drive, which leads to
Navy Pier on the lake (page 30).

Kids will enjoy seeing the dramatic Centennial
Fountain (located on the north bank between
Michigan Avenue and Lake Shore Drive) that

shoots an arc of water almost across the river. The
State Street Bridge Gallery in the lower level of the
southeast tower of the State Street Bridge stages
three art exhibitions each summer. Viewing the art
may not thrill the youngsters in your group, but
seeing the gigantic gears that operate the draw-
bridge will.

SEASONS AND TIMES
➤ State Street Bridge Gallery: May—mid-Oct, Mon—Sat, 10 am—7 pm;
Sun, 10 am—5 pm. Not much happens along the river during the winter
because it's too cold.

COST
➤ State Street Bridge Gallery: Free. The walkways are public paths.

GETTING THERE
➤ The Chicago River meanders from Lake Michigan through the city.
The areas described above are on the East Branch of the river between
street numbers 300 and 400 N.
➤ By car, take Michigan Ave. north until you come to the river. Pay
parking is available in several garages and small lots nearby. About 5
minutes from Grant Park.
➤ By public transit, El stops near the river include Merchandise Mart
(Brown and Purple lines), Grand Ave. (Red line), State & Lake and
Clark & Lake (Green, Brown, Purple, and Orange lines).

NEARBY
➤ Navy Pier, Hancock Observatory, The Magnificent Mile.

COMMENT
➤ On St. Patrick's Day, head to the river and watch organizers dye the
river green. No stroller or wheelchair accessibility at most points. No
water fountains or public restrooms.

Fun in the Field
THE FIELD MUSEUM

**1400 S. Lake Shore Dr., Chicago
(312) 922-9410
www.fmnh.org**

Boasting mummies, dinosaur bones and lots of interesting displays, The Field Museum is a treasure-trove of fascinating artifacts. At the back of the main hall, the *Tyrannosaurus Rex* affectionately named Sue bares her huge teeth at visitors. Other dinosaurs engage in mock battle in the Life Over Time exhibit, where hands-on activities will teach everyone how life developed on earth.

The Underground Adventure exhibit is a hit with anyone who loves bugs. First it shrinks visitors down to insect size, then transports them underground to meet grubs and worms and other subterranean creatures. In Exploring Ancient Egypt, you can tour a burial tomb, view bona fide mummies and ogle the buried treasures. Children enjoy playing among the realistic depiction of ancient Egyptian life at the end of the exhibit.

Culture is celebrated at The Field Museum with captivating displays that explore Africa, Asia and Native American lands. The museum has plenty of preserved specimens to view, ranging from delicate butterflies to enormous elephants.

Learning programs, overnight adventures and guided field trips make this museum a rich resource of educational entertainment for your whole family.

SEASONS AND TIMES
➤ Summer (May 22–Sept 4): Daily, 8 am–5 pm. Winter (Sept 5– May 21): Daily, 9 am–5 pm. Closed Christmas and New Year's.

COST
➤ Adults $8, seniors, students with ID and children (3 to 11) $4, tots under 3, teachers and military with ID free. Extra ticket required for Underground Adventure: Adults $4, seniors $3, students with ID and children (3 to 11) and $2. Free on Wednesdays. Memberships available.

GETTING THERE
➤ By car, take Columbus Dr. south to McFetridge Dr. Turn east onto the Museum Campus. The Field Museum will be on the north side. Park in any of the pay lots east of the museum, or on the street. About 5 minutes from Grant Park.
➤ By public transit, take CTA bus 6 (Jeffrey Express) on State St. to the corner of Roosevelt Rd. and Columbus. The museum is a short walk east through the Museum Campus.

COMMENT
➤ The Field Museum is gigantic and younger kids will tire after 1 to 2 hours.

Chicago's Heart
GRANT PARK/LAKEFRONT

**Bounded by Michigan Ave., Lake Shore Dr., Randolph St.
and Roosevelt Rd., Chicago
(312) 747-2474
www.chicagoparkdistrict.com**

No visit to Chicago is complete without a stop at Grant Park and the lakefront. Comprising 319 acres, Grant Park is at the center of 24 miles of Lake Michigan shoreline, forever protected from development by the city's early leaders. With lush formal gardens, tree-lined lawns and lots of pathways for strolling, it's a peaceful refuge in the heart of the city. Buckingham Fountain in the middle of the park is a popular gathering spot for regular visitors and newcomers alike, who come to gaze at its water sprays that project an eye-popping 135 feet into the air. If you visit on a summer evening, you can see the fountain colorfully lit. Grant Park has other attractions, such as free concerts in the Petrillo Bandshell and the Taste of Chicago, a giant food festival that draws thousands to the site in early July.

You'll find Lake Michigan due east of Grant Park, across Lake Shore Drive. Take the kids there to watch the sailboats bobbing in Monroe Harbor. Ducks are always looking for handouts along the shore. From here, you can follow the lakefront path south to the Museum Campus or north to Navy Pier (page 30) and beyond.

SEASONS AND TIMES
➤ Park: Year-round, daily. Buckingham Fountain: May 1—Oct 1 (light show runs from dusk until 11 pm).

COST
➤ Free.

GETTING THERE
➤ By car, take Lake Shore Dr. or Michigan Ave. to Jackson St., Monroe St., or Balbo St., all of which cut through Grant Park. Pay parking available at underground garages at the corners of Monroe and Columbus Ave., Michigan and Van Buren St., and Michigan and Monroe, as well as on the street.
➤ By public transit, take any of the CTA buses that run along Michigan to Grant Park. Or take any of the El lines that circle the Loop and get off at Adams St. or Madison St. and walk east to the park.
➤ By bicycle, follow the lakefront path.

NEARBY
➤ The Art Institute of Chicago, Museum Campus.

COMMENT
➤ Grant Park is the perfect stopping place to rest or have a picnic between visits to the museums.

See it From Above
HANCOCK OBSERVATORY

875 N. Michigan Ave., Chicago
1-888-875-8439
www.hancock-observatory.com

Seeing Chicago from the Hancock Observatory, 94 stories above the ground, is a great way to grasp the awesome size of the city and the grandeur of Lake Michigan. Kids' jaws drop as they survey the tiny cars on the streets below, the beaches that unfurl along the lakefront and the buildings and houses that spread to the horizon. Pay $1 to see things close up with high-power binoculars designed to describe the sights as you look at them.

One part of the observatory is enclosed in screen, so you can experience the weather at 1,000 feet above ground. You can climb into a window washer's pulley cart that's set up inside to imagine what it's like to wash the tower windows. Children naturally gravitate towards the observatory's two banks of computers. They contain simple games for small kids and in-depth information about the tower's construction for older visitors. Archival photos with captions are displayed on one wall and offer a concise history of Chicago. To impress the folks back home, take a photo of your kids having lunch on a steel beam that appears to be hanging over the city, courtesy of a clever backdrop.

SEASONS AND TIMES
➤ Year-round: Daily, 9 am—midnight.

COST
➤ Adults $8.75, seniors $6.75, children (5 to 17) $6, under 5 free.

GETTING THERE
➤ By car, take Michigan Ave. north over the Chicago River and continue on to the tower. Pay parking is available in the tower's garage. Enter on Chestnut St. or Delaware St. About 5 minutes from Grant Park.
➤ By public transit, take any of the CTA buses traveling north on Michigan to the John Hancock Center.

NEARBY
➤ The Magnificent Mile.

COMMENT
➤ The views are astounding, but a 30- to 45-minute visit will be enough for most kids.

SIMILAR ATTRACTION
➤ **Sears Tower—The Skydeck.** It may not hold the "world's tallest" title anymore, but the Skydeck still towers over anything else in Chicago. 23 S. Wacker Dr., Chicago (312) 875-9696. www.the-skydeck.com

Art on Foot
LOOP SCULPTURES

Various plazas in downtown Chicago

Chicago is home to thousands of accomplished artists, with examples of their work displayed in plazas and parks around the city. Since children are often the most enthusiastic admirers of sculptures, why not pack a picnic lunch and take them on a walking tour of the Loop where they can see some of the city's best.

The most popular is the untitled sculpture by Picasso in the Daley Center Plaza, located on Washington Street between Clark Street and Dearborn Street. It resembles a giant bird and in fine weather kids use its broad, sloped "belly" as a gigantic slide. The water fountain and picnic tables make this plaza a preferred lunch stop. Kitty corner from the Daley Center (to the northwest) in the James R. Thompson Center Plaza (100 W. Randolph St.), is the *Monument with Standing Beast*. This black and white sculptural group, inspired by a series of doodles by artist Jean DuBuffet, is ideal for a youngster's game of hide-and-seek or tag.

Flamingo, by Alexander Calder, resembles a giant orange squid standing on its tentacles in the Federal Center Plaza at Adams Street and Dearborn. Everyone will be awed by its hulking presence. For sheer beauty and pleasurable surroundings, you can't beat Marc Chagall's *Four Seasons* in the First National Bank Plaza at Dearborn and Monroe. This colorful mosaic, guarded by small shade trees, is situated a flight of stairs above a large fountain and features plenty of spots to sit and take a breather.

SEASONS AND TIMES

→ Year-round: Daily.

COST

→ Free.

GETTING THERE

→ All of the sculptures described above are located in the Loop.

→ By car, take Michigan Ave. north to Randolph St. Turn west and drive to Clark St. then go south on Clark to Washington St. Pay parking is available in several garages nearby. Minutes from Grant Park.

→ By public transit, almost every El line passes through the Loop. The closest stations to the Daley Center Plaza are Washington on the Blue line (walk west to Daley Center) and Washington on the Brown, Purple and Orange lines (walk east to Daley Center).

NEARBY

→ Sears Tower.

COMMENT

→ On any given day you'll see demonstrators, street performers and other interesting folk milling about on the plazas around the sculptures.

Kid-fun Shopping
THE MAGNIFICENT MILE

Michigan Ave. (from Chicago Ave. to Lake Shore Dr.), Chicago

Chicago is known for fine shopping. The Magnificent Mile, Chicago's most famous shopping strip, boasts stores offering the latest from hi-tech gadgetry to camping gear and more.

Venerable FAO Schwarz (840 N. Michigan Ave.; 312-587-5000) is a three-story toy store that's packed with every imaginable plaything. A transplant from New York, FAO Schwarz is what toy stores look like in kids' dreams, complete with lots of lights, bells and colorful decorations. Watch the giant steel balls travel down the Rube Goldberg-like contraption on your way up the escalators. Ensure you don't miss the "floor pianos" on the second and third levels.

For doll-lovers, American Girl Place (111 E. Chicago Ave.; 312-943-9400) is a must-see. Based on the famous line of American Girl dolls, this retailer is a high-class purveyor of figurines as well as books, clothing and all the accessories. The Café caters to young shoppers and their dolls, with special seats designed for the faux tykes (reservations required). Don't forget to take in the American Girl musical revue at the Theater that is located in the store.

Plan to spend a few minutes at the Chicago Water Works (168 E. Pearson Ave.; 312-744-2400), across the street from the famous Water Tower. Built in 1867, this pumping station still serves the surrounding area. The Visitor Center inside offers brochures describing every conceivable Chicago tourist attraction. The City of Chicago Store is packed with retired city street signs, parking meters and other items turned into unique collectibles.

SEASONS AND TIMES
➤ FAO Schwarz: Year-round, Mon—Thu, 10 am—8 pm; Fri—Sat, 10 am—9 pm; Sun, 10 am—6 pm. Closed Thanksgiving, Christmas and Easter. American Girl Place: Year-round, Mon—Sat, 9:30 am— 9 pm; Sun, 10 am—7 pm. Holiday hours vary. Chicago Water Works (Visitor Center): Year-round, daily, 7:30 am—7 pm. (City of Chicago Store): Year-round, Mon—Sat, 9:30 am—5 pm; Sun, 11 am—5 pm. Both closed Thanksgiving, Christmas and New Year's.

GETTING THERE
➤ By car, take Michigan Ave. north until you cross the bridge over the Chicago River. Pay parking available in several lots and garages off the side streets. About 5 minutes from Grant Park.
➤ By public transit, take the Red line El to Grand Ave. or Chicago Ave., then walk east to Michigan. Or take any of the CTA buses that travel along Michigan.

NEARBY
➤ Navy Pier, Chicago River, Hancock Observatory.

COMMENT
➤ Restaurants along The Magnificent Mile offer takeout and sit-down dining. During the holiday season, kids love to see the fanciful windows in Marshall Field's State Street Department Store (111 N. State St.), south of the Chicago River.

Ahoy, Matey
NAVY PIER

600 E. Grand Ave., Chicago
(312) 595-5300
www.navypier.com

For a dose of concentrated family fun, it's hard to beat Navy Pier. This popular waterfront destination features carnival rides, live entertainment, curio shops, restaurants and other diversions for whiling away an afternoon.

Older kids will definitely want to ride the giant Ferris wheel, which provides awesome views of Chicago and Lake Michigan. The carousel, with its menagerie of animals, is a hit with smaller children. There are lots of interesting sights to take in along the south side of the pier, from giant sailing ships to street performers. Rent a four-person quadcycle near the west end of the pier for some enjoyable lakefront sightseeing. In winter, bring ice skates and take a few turns on the outdoor rink. Skate rentals are available.

Inside Navy Pier, let your kids romp about the fountains and lush greenery in Crystal Gardens, a one-acre oasis that's a perfect haven during the colder months. In the main corridor you'll find dozens of charming shops, full of tourist and kid-friendly goods. Eat at the extensive food court or visit one of six sit-down restaurants for a fancier meal.

A resident acting troupe offers near continuous entertainment for kids throughout the year with special stage shows around Halloween and Christmas. Navy Pier also houses an IMAX™ Theater and the Chicago Children's Museum (page 17).

SEASONS AND TIMES
➤ Summer (Early May—Sept 6): Sun—Thu, 10 am—10 pm; Fri—Sat, 10 am—midnight. Fall (Sept 7—Oct 31): Mon—Thu, 10 am—9 pm; Fri—Sat, 10 am—11 pm; Sun, 10 am—7 pm. Winter (Nov—Apr): Mon—Thu, 10 am—8 pm; Fri—Sat, 10 am— 10 pm; Sun, 10 am—7 pm.

COST
➤ It's free to visit the pier and Crystal Gardens. There are fees for the IMAX™ Theater, rides and other attractions.

GETTING THERE
➤ By car, take Lake Shore Dr. north to the Illinois St. Exit. Go east on Illinois and follow the signs to Navy Pier. Pay parking available in garages on the pier. About 5 minutes from Grant Park.
➤ By public transit, take CTA bus 29 (State St.) or 65 (Grand Ave.) to the pier's front entrance. A free trolley travels between Navy Pier and State. Board the bus beside the "Navy Pier Trolley Stop" sign.
➤ By bicycle, take the lakefront path directly to Navy Pier.

NEARBY
➤ Ohio St. Beach, lakefront path.

COMMENT
➤ Navy Pier can be an all-day affair, but plan at least a 3-hour visit.

CHAPTER 2

MUSEUMS

Introduction

C hicago is full of museums, reflecting everything from the city's role in industry to its
rich ethnic diversity. Check out the Chicago
Historical Society for local history, or visit the First
Division Museum for a moving tour through the great
wars of the 20th century. These museums aren't
dusty repositories of old artifacts—they are experiential centers where children can learn about
science, nature, immigrants, medicine, communications and culture. Most have areas specifically
designed to accommodate children's eager hands
and vivid imaginations.

Many of these museums also offer excellent
dining opportunities allowing you to make your visit
a full-day outing, especially if it's rainy or cold.

NOTE
The following museums, which are covered elsewhere in this guide,
also welcome children:
The Art Institute of Chicago (Chapter 1, page 15)
Chicago Children's Museum (Chapter 1, page 17)
The Field Museum (Chapter 1, page 21)

Atten-shun!
FIRST DIVISION MUSEUM AT CANTIGNY

I S. 151 Winfield Rd., Wheaton
(630) 668-5185

Military buffs get their fill at this museum while learning the history of the U.S. First Infantry Division. This military unit is also known as the Big Red One on account of the red numeral 1 in its logo.

Your first stop is the row of armored tanks and cannons, dating from World War I to the Vietnam War, that guard the entrance to the building. After your kids have clambered over the military hardware, head indoors where they can experience life as a combat soldier. You won't find boring displays of dusty rifles here—this museum, which caters to children's penchants for hands-on action, takes visitors to the battleground and puts them right into the action.

In the World War I section, you'll learn about the brutal life on the front lines as you walk through a re-created trench. Overhead, sounds of exploding shells fill the air as soldiers prepare to scramble over the top. In the World War II display, you can board a landing craft heading for the beaches of Normandy. Old film footage will show you the carnage that took place there during the D-Day invasion. When the screen opens, you'll crash the beaches themselves on D-Day Plus One. Elsewhere, a jungle scene recounts the Big Red One's action in Vietnam, and a few display cases cover the unit's involvement in Operation Desert Storm.

The First Division Museum is just one feature of Cantigny Park, which comprises 500 acres of groomed grounds and gardens. Older children and adults might enjoy taking the guided tour at the Robert R. McCormick mansion.

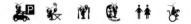

SEASONS AND TIMES
→ Mar–Memorial Day: Tue–Sun, 10 am–4 pm. Memorial Day–Labor Day: Tue–Sun, 10 am–5 pm. Labor Day–late Dec: Tue–Sun, 10 am–4 pm. Feb: Fri–Sun, 10 am–4 pm. Closed all major holidays.

COST
→ Free.

GETTING THERE
→ By car, take the I-290 and go west to I-88 W. Continue west on I-88 until the Winfield Dr. N. Exit, and follow Winfield for about 3 miles. Look for the Cantigny sign. Pay parking on site ($5). About 45 minutes from Grant Park.

NEARBY
→ DuPage Children's Museum.

COMMENT
→ Plan at least a 1-hour visit at the museum itself and another hour for exploring Cantigny Park.

Reliving the Past
CHICAGO HISTORICAL
SOCIETY

1601 N. Clark St., Chicago
(312) 642-4600
www.chicagohs.org

C hicago has a rich and colorful history and the Chicago Historical Society is packed with artifacts that tell you about it.

At the Chicago History Wing, kids can hop aboard Chicago's first steam engine and pretend they are locomotive engineers. They can examine the city's original fire engine and watch a short film on the 1871 Chicago Fire. If sports are more to your liking, be sure to see the uniforms, trophies and other memorabilia from Chicago's greatest teams. When youngsters start to fidget, steer them to the exhibits in the Hands-On History Gallery. They can imagine they're fur trappers or listen to radio shows their grandparents used to hear. Hours are irregular in this exhibit, so call ahead to avoid disappointment. The Chicago Dioramas gallery offers visitors a brief and miniaturized synopsis of city history using tiny figurines and buildings.

American history is on display in the museum, with examinations of the Revolutionary War, slavery and the Civil War. Downstairs in the Illinois Pioneer Life Gallery, kids will be amazed to see what hardships the area's early settlers had to endure. Occasionally, museum staff show visitors how pioneers performed daily chores, such as spinning flax and weaving yarn.

Before you head home, walk about the museum grounds and locate the tomb—the last remains of a pioneer cemetery once occupying Lincoln Park.

SEASONS AND TIMES
➤ Year-round: Mon—Sat, 9:30 am—4:30 pm; Sun, noon—5 pm. Closed Thanksgiving, Christmas and New Year's.

COST
➤ Adults $5, seniors and youths (13 to 22) $3, children (6 to 12) $1, under 6 free. Free on Mondays.

GETTING THERE
➤ By car, take Lake Shore Dr. north to the LaSalle/North Ave Exit. Travel west on LaSalle to the garage on the corner of LaSalle and Clark St. About 15 minutes from Grant Park.
➤ By public transit, take CTA bus 22 (Clark St.). If you're in the Loop, board on Dearborn St. In the summer, a free trolley runs between Sedgwick El (Brown line) and the museum.
➤ By bicycle or on foot, take the lakefront path to the bridge that crosses over Lake Shore north of North Ave. and go west to the corner of North and Clark.

NEARBY
➤ Lincoln Park Zoo, North Ave. Beach.

COMMENT
➤ Plan at least a 1-hour visit.

The Black American Experience
DUSABLE MUSEUM OF AFRICAN-AMERICAN HISTORY

**740 E. 56th Place, Chicago
(773) 947-0600
www.dusablemuseum.org**

The DuSable Museum goes a long way towards defining the experiences and historical achievements of black Americans. While the displays themselves are mainly narrative and geared to school-aged children, younger kids still enjoy the visit.

The Fight to Fly: Blacks in Aviation exhibit will especially interest anyone who likes airplanes. Featuring photos and stories of America's black aviators, it also has personal belongings of the pioneers, including Major Robert H. Lawrence, America's first black astronaut, and Bessie Coleman, the first African-American pilot.

Elsewhere, a display on slavery is both vivid and disturbing. While eye-opening for children who have learned about America's slave legacy in classrooms, those under eight may be frightened by the frank presentation of the subject matter. So, take them to see the re-created office of Harold Washington, Chicago's first black mayor, or visit the abundant African and African-American art found through-out the museum.

The DuSable Museum sponsors a full calendar of on-going events, including DuSable After Dark, which is a series of social networking events for young adults and the Film Review Club for movie buffs.

SEASONS AND TIMES
➤ Year-round: Daily, 10 am—5 pm. Closed Thanksgiving, Christmas and New Year's.

COST
➤ Adults $3, seniors and students $2, youths (6 to 13) $1, under 6 free. Free on Sundays.

GETTING THERE
➤ By car, take Lake Shore Dr. south to the 57th St. Exit. Follow 57th west as it curves around the Museum of Science and Industry and becomes Cornell Dr., then turn west onto Midway Plaisance. Take it to Cottage Grove Ave. and turn north. Go 2 blocks to 57th and travel west. The free parking lot will be on the north side. About 30 minutes from Grant Park.

NEARBY
➤ Museum of Science and Industry, University of Chicago.

COMMENT
➤ Do a tour of the University of Chicago's gothic campus after the museum. Plan a 1-hour visit.

Adjust Your Antenna
MUSEUM OF BROADCAST COMMUNICATIONS

78 E. Washington St., Chicago
(312) 629-6000
www.mbcnet.org

You know you're in for a treat the minute you step inside this museum which offers visitors a fun romp through the history of broadcast communications. Its walls are lined with old radios and TVs that fascinate kids who are used to viewing 24-inch color screens and larger.

A series of small rooms in the radio section depict living rooms and kitchens in radio's heyday, from 1920 to the '50s. Walk into each room and a show from that era starts playing from the radio. In one corner, kids can tune old radios to the Lone Ranger, Little Orphan Annie and other old-time favorite shows to hear what grandpa used to listen to when he came home from school. Display cases filled with memorabilia, such as decoder rings and sheriff badges, reveal how much fun children had listening to programs in radio's golden age. Kids can even open Fibber McGee's closet (fortunately, its contents don't spill out!).

In the television section, you can examine ancient television cameras and other equipment and even check out classic TV commercials. Don't miss the

Commercial Break Gift Shop with its recordings of old radio shows and other related trinkets.

After the visit, explore the Chicago Cultural Center that houses the museum, where you can enjoy browsing the art galleries and sipping coffee in the pleasant lobby.

SEASONS AND TIMES
➤ Year-round: Mon—Sat, 10 am—4:30 pm; Sun, noon—5 pm. Closed all holidays.

COST
➤ Free.

GETTING THERE
➤ By car, take Michigan Ave. north to Washington St. Pay parking is available in several garages in the neighborhood. About 5 minutes from Grant Park.
➤ By public transit, take the Orange, Purple, Green or Brown El lines to Wabash/Randolph and walk 1 block east on Randolph to the Cultural Center. Or take any of the CTA buses traveling along Michigan and get off at Washington.

NEARBY
➤ The Art Institute of Chicago, Grant Park.

COMMENT
➤ The Museum of Broadcast Communications also houses the A.C. Nielsen Jr. On-line Research Center, with 70,000 hours of radio and television programming on-line. Plan a 1-hour visit.

More than Science
MUSEUM OF SCIENCE AND INDUSTRY

**57th St. and Lake Shore Dr., Chicago
(773) 684-1414
www.msichicago.org**

F
ew places in Chicago can match the fascinating array of attractions and exhibits found at the Museum of Science and Industry. Even young children enjoy walking through U-505, a genuine German submarine that's permanently docked on the museum's east-side. Preserved as she was when Allied forces captured her in 1944, the boat offers visitors a hands-on look at a submariner's life during World War II. Another must-see exhibit is the Coal Mine that takes you on an underground train for a look at how coal is mined.

Perhaps you prefer traveling above ground. At The Transportation Zone, kids can examine a real Boeing 747 suspended from the ceiling and the Empire 999, a locomotive that was the first vehicle to break the 100-mile per hour barrier. The Lunar Module trainer used by Apollo astronauts to prepare for moon missions and Aurora 7, the Mercury space capsule that circled the globe in 1962, are also displayed.

Opportunities to learn science fundamentals abound at the museum. The Whispering Gallery uses parabolic dishes to demonstrate the principles of sound travel. The giant Walk-Through Heart reveals the workings of this vital organ.

Even kids who are not interested in science will find endless adventures at this museum. However, the visit is better suited for those older than five, who can grasp the significance of the exhibits.

SEASONS AND TIMES
➤ Summer (Memorial Day—Labor Day): Daily, 9:30 am—5:30 pm. Winter: Mon—Fri, 9:30 am—4 pm; Sat—Sun, 9:30 am—5 pm.

COST
➤ Adults $7, seniors $6, children (3 to 11) $3.50, under 3 free. Free on Thursdays. Additional fees for special exhibits.

GETTING THERE
➤ By car, take Lake Shore Dr. south to the 57th St. Exit and travel east. Follow the curve around to the west side of the museum and turn into the underground pay parking garage ($7). About 15 minutes from Grant Park.
➤ By public transit, take CTA bus 10 (Museum of Science and Industry) from State St. in the Loop to the museum. It runs daily during the summer and on weekends for the remainder of the year.

NEARBY
➤ DuSable Museum of African American History, University of Chicago.

COMMENT
➤ Children older than 10 will want to spend 3 or 4 hours here, but younger kids will get their fill in a shorter time.

Nature on Display
PEGGY NOTEBAERT NATURE MUSEUM

2430 N. Cannon Dr., Chicago
(773) 755-5100
www.chias.org/museum

Nature-loving kids—is there any other type— flock to the Peggy Notebaert Nature Museum. This two-year-old museum explores the natural history of the Midwest with hands-on exhibits ranging from how water flows to what pests live in your house. The biggest attraction is the Judy Istock Butterfly Haven. In this glass-walled room, hundreds of colorful butterflies fly freely. If you're lucky, one might land on you. Kids can examine up close the dazzling insects and chrysalis waiting to hatch. Signs and knowledgeable docents help visitors identify the insects.

At the Children's Gallery, kids learn about ecosystems found in the Chicago area by playing in tunnels under a fake prairie, crawling into a beaver lodge or catching fish in an artificial pond. Wilderness Walk has preserved animals and plants, examples of species that once flourished here. City Science, another popular exhibit, is a 3,000-square-foot, two-story house whose cutaway walls reveal the variety of creatures that commonly inhabit homes, from spiders in the basement to microbes in the bathroom. Fifty computers throughout the museum are connected to the Internet and loaded with software that provides a guided tour through an environmental crisis.

Leave some time to explore the grounds outside, which emulate Illinois prairies packed with wild flowers and other native plants. Immediately west of the museum, North Pond is home to a flock of ducks.

The museum sponsors educational programs for adults and children, such as the Knee-High Naturalists program where four-and five-year-olds meet weekly for some hands-on science fun.

SEASONS AND TIMES
→ Year-round: Daily, 10 am—6 pm (Wed until 8 pm). Closed Thanksgiving, Christmas and New Year's.

COST
→ Adults $6, seniors and students $4, children $3.

GETTING THERE
→ By car, take Lake Shore Dr. north to the Fullerton Ave. Exit. Travel west on Fullerton to Cannon Dr. The museum is on the northwest corner. You can park in the Lincoln Park Zoo lot, just south of the intersection on Cannon for $7, or try to find street parking. About 30 minutes from Grant Park.
→ By public transit, take the Brown or Red El line to Fullerton. On summer weekends, a free trolley operates from this station to the museum. Otherwise, you'll have to walk east along Fullerton for about a mile.
→ By bicycle, follow the lakefront path until Fullerton. Then head west to Cannon.

NEARBY
→ Lincoln Park Zoo, North Ave. Beach.

COMMENT
→ The Butterfly Café on the museum's second floor serves tasty lunches that are matched only by the views of the surrounding nature. Plan a 1.5-hour visit.

Honoring the Downtrodden
FEET FIRST EXHIBIT
SCHOLL COLLEGE OF
PODIATRIC MEDICINE

1001 N. Dearborn St., Chicago
(312) 280-2487
www.scholl.edu/e/index.htm

Y ou might not think about them often, but your feet are your servants. They support your entire weight every day and rarely complain. The Feet First Exhibit at the Scholl College of Podiatric Medicine finally gives these loyal dogs the recognition they deserve.

This charming, tiny two-room museum has enough hands-on features to keep most kids engaged until they've learned more about their feet than you knew at their age. The first room is devoted to the feet themselves. Kids can pretend they're shoe salespersons-cum-X-ray-technicians by pushing the buttons on a foot X-ray machine. Shoe stores once used these machines to ensure customers got fitted for their proper shoe size. Among the room's other exhibits, kids can probe and poke the giant foot skeleton. Explanatory panels describe the significance of the displays.

The second room is full of Dr. Scholl memorabilia. In the early 1900s, Dr. William Mathias Scholl, a bona fide doctor, founded this podiatry college and the now-famous footwear company that bears his name. You can watch vintage Dr. Scholl television commercials and a short film that was used to train the company's sales staff. Everyone will enjoy listening to the recordings of songs sung by conventioneers at Dr. Scholl conventions. Don't miss the shoe exhibit in the hallway outside the museum. Among the jaw-dropping displays is a size 35 shoe that belonged to the world's tallest man.

SEASONS AND TIMES
➻ Year-round: Mon—Fri, 9 am—4 pm. Closed holidays.

COST
➻ Free.

GETTING THERE
➻ By car, take Dearborn St. north over the river and cross Chicago Ave. Scholl College is on the northeast corner of Dearborn and Oak St. Limited street parking is available. The Feet First Exhibit is behind and to the right of the reception desk. About 20 minutes from Grant Park.
➻ By public transit, take the El (Red line) to Clark/Division. Walk 1 block east on Division to Dearborn, then turn south and walk 3 blocks to the Scholl College.

NEARBY
➻ The Magnificent Mile, Washington Square Park, Newberry Library.

COMMENT
➻ The museum's exhibits take about 30 minutes to see, so plan to include a visit to historic Washington Square Park, which is kitty corner to the southwest.

Knightly Kids
THE BALZEKAS MUSEUM OF LITHUANIAN CULTURE

6500 S. Pulaski Rd., Chicago
(773) 582-6500

Knights, castles and horses are what many kids dream of and Lithuanian history is full of them. Kids can tap into this history and imagine themselves as little knights at the Balzekas Museum.

Young visitors have the most fun in the Children's Museum of Immigrant History at Balzekas. The first half of this two-room section reveals the life of rural Lithuanians from the early 20th century. A miniature farmhouse, complete with furniture and farmyard animals, keeps little hands occupied while revealing the simple lifestyle of Lithuanian peasants. Featured, too, is a collection of common household implements, a stringed musical instrument called a kankles that kids can strum, a swinging cradle and other hands-on artifacts.

Cross a wooden bridge into the second room and Lithuania's martial history comes alive. This castle-like space is filled with dress-up and role-playing opportunities. A collection of hats, helmets and weaponry puts youngsters into a knightly mood. They can ride a wooden horse, assemble a giant jigsaw puzzle of a knight, or put their faces in holes in a painting of a knight on horseback.

The rest of the museum is designed for adults, but some children might enjoy looking at the historic objects, which include amber jewelry, ancient weapons, old documents and other relics of Lithuania's past. Paintings and photos occupy the second floor.

SEASONS AND TIMES
➤ Year-round: Daily, 10 am—4 pm. Closed on major holidays.

COST
➤ Adults $3, seniors and students $2, under 12 $1.

GETTING THERE
➤ By car, take I-90/94 or Lake Shore Dr. south to I-55 S. Take I-55 S. to the Pulaski Rd. Exit and travel south on Pulaski past 63rd St. The museum is in a long, two-story building on the west side of the street. On-street parking is generally available. About 30 minutes from Grant Park.

NEARBY
➤ Midway Airport.

COMMENT
➤ A visit to Balzekas is a good time to remind your kids about the role immigrants played in building America. The museum is not just a collection of artifacts; it's also a meeting place for Chicago's vibrant Lithuanian community. Plan a 1-hour visit.

Other Museums

The Peace Museum

314 W. Institute Place, Chicago
(312) 440-1860
www.peacemuseum.org

This museum contains over 10,000 works of art and artifacts from the peace movement. Each year, this museum holds four exhibitions incorporating works from this collection. Recent exhibitions have included The Unforgettable Fire & the A-Bomb and Humanity and Peace on Earth: Interfaith Approaches to Peace.

➤ Year-round: Sat, 11 am—5 pm and by special appointment. These hours are subject to change, so call ahead.

➤ Individuals $3.50, child under 12 $2.

Museum of Holography/Chicago

1134 W. Washington Blvd., Chicago
(312) 226-1007
www.holographiccenter.com/museum1.htm

Holograms, those popular three-dimensional images, are the focus of this museum and research center. Visitors can see an array of state-of-the-art holograms, such as Michael Jordan appearing to fly in mid-air and a crawling tarantula.

➤ Year-round: Wed—Sun, 12:30 pm—5 pm.

➤ Individuals $2.50, under 6 free.

International Museum of Surgical Science

1524 N. Lake Shore Dr., Chicago
(312) 642-6502
www.imss.org

Surgery through the centuries is explained in this museum through paintings and a collection of surgical tools and implements. Children interested in medicine will find it educational, but its somewhat graphic content may disturb those under 12.

➤ Year-round: Tue—Sat, 10 am—4 pm.

➤ Adults $5, seniors and students $3.

CHAPTER 3

IN YOUR
NEIGHBORHOOD

Introduction

Parents living in Chicago, the city of neighborhoods, don't need to travel far to find attractions and activities to entertain kids. Some of the best places are in their own neighborhood and cost very little or nothing at all.

This chapter contains a variety of ideas for outings to public markets, painting studios, craft shops and other everyday places where a little imagination can turn an ordinary trip into a fun-filled adventure. Children's libraries and bookstores are great places for kids to explore. For more action, take them bowling or ice skating. Looking for places where the kids can blow off steam? Then you'll want to investigate Chicago's outstanding play lots, pools and park districts.

Crafty Places
ARTS AND CRAFTS INSTRUCTION

Is your little one an aspiring Van Gogh? Then let his or her talent blossom in an arts or crafts class.

Numerous neighborhood organizations sponsor these creative outlets and offer courses ranging from fingerpainting, to weaving, to bead jewelry creation. Community organizations often lead the way in arts courses. The Hyde Park Arts Center features a broad range of classes for youth in painting, drawing, ceramics and other disciplines. Even tots get in on the action with multi-media courses for ages two to five. The Evanston Art Center is another outstanding place, offering over 100 different courses. The Chicago Park District and Suburban Park Districts also have arts and craft courses for children, lasting a day to several weeks.

Don't forget the museums. Many, including the Art Institute (page 15) and the Museum of Contemporary Art (MCA), have a wide selection of art classes for kids. Recent courses at the MCA have included Creative Crowns: Wacky Hats and Hair-Raising Wigs, where six- to eight-year-olds craft headpieces inspired by children's stories and folklore. Another fun class, Wearable Art, teaches 9- to 11-year olds how to decorate clothing. The MCA also sponsors a series of free one-day family workshops.

If your kids like jewelry, they might enjoy a course at a bead shop. Bead In Hand in Oak Park welcomes children as young as six to its classes. Caravan Beads in Chicago is another option, though their classes are geared for individuals 12 and up.

ART INSTITUTE
111 S. Michigan Ave., Chicago (312) 443-3600
www.artic.edu

BEAD IN HAND
145 Harrison St., Oak Park (708) 848-1761
www.beadinhand.com

CARAVAN BEADS
3361 N. Lincoln Ave., Chicago (773) 248-9555
www.caravanchicago.com

CHICAGO PARK DISTRICT
(312) 742-PLAY (7529); www.chicagoparkdistrict.com

EVANSTON ART CENTER
2603 Sheridan Rd., Evanston (847) 475-5300
www.evanstonartcenter.org

HYDE PARK ART CENTER
5307 S. Hyde Park Ave., Chicago (773) 324-5520
www.hydeparkart.org

MUSEUM OF CONTEMPORARY ART
220 E. Chicago Ave., Chicago (312) 280-2660
www.mcachicago.org

Rainy Days
BOWLING ALLEYS

Strike! Is there any better way to beat the bad weather blahs? Bowling is an ideal outing for children of all ages, as well as their parents. Toddlers have fun rolling the ball, even if they play by their own rules. More than just fun— it's inexpensive. A whole family can enjoy a few games for under $20 (including shoe rentals). There is no shortage of bowling alleys in Chicago. Visit www.metromix.com for a comprehensive list. Most alleys offer instruction, leagues for every level, and host special and seasonal events. Have you thought about having your child's next birthday at the lanes? A bowling party is a great way to celebrate with friends.

If you have older children, a regular lane and a lightweight ball are all you need for a good time. If your family includes smaller children, consider a game of bumper bowling. Gutter pads enable even the smallest bowler to get the ball to the pins. Call before you go and find out which family activities are available.

Probably the most popular downtown alley for families is the state-of-the-art, 36-lane Marina City Lanes in the House of Blues complex. Waveland Bowl on the North Side features a Kids Theater (supervised), where youngsters tired of bowling can watch videos. In the suburbs, check out Tivoli Bowl in Downers Grove. This family-oriented alley has four lanes devoted to bumper bowling and three private party rooms.

MARINA CITY LANES
330 N. State St., Chicago (312) 644-0300

WAVELAND BOWL
3700 N. Western Ave., Chicago (773) 472-5900
www.wavelandbowl.com

TIVOLI BOWL
938 Warren Ave., Downers Grove (630) 969-0660
www.tivolibowl.com

Book 'em, Dano!
CHILDREN'S LIBRARIES AND BOOKSTORES

Kids love books! And the Chicago-area libraries and bookstores are great places to indulge them. The king of children's libraries is the Thomas Hughes Children's Library at the Harold Washington Library. This 18,000-square-foot facility contains 120,000 volumes of children's literature, ranging from picture to reference books. Books are just the beginning. The library also houses 70 children's periodicals, a natural history collection and a computer center with a dozen computers with Internet access plus two multimedia computers. While few other libraries match the magnitude of Hughes, most offer a comfortable, inviting place for children to read or be read to. Chicago Public Libraries are found in nearly every neighborhood in Chicago. For their locations and operating hours, visit www.chipublib.org. Communities neighboring Chicago operate their own library systems.

Children's bookstores also cater to kids who read. Children in Paradise, located downtown, has an awesome selection of kids' books, software, CDs and other products in a warm, fun atmosphere. Women & Children First on Clark Street is best known for its feminist literature, but it has a well-stocked children's section as well. In the western suburbs, check out the Magic Tree Book Store in Oak Park. Staff are knowledgeable and friendly, and there is a cozy reading area.

**THOMAS HUGHES CHILDREN'S LIBRARY
(HAROLD WASHINGTON LIBRARY)**
400 S. State St., Chicago (312) 747-4200;
www.chipublib.org

CHILDREN IN PARADISE
909 N. Rush St., Chicago (312) 951-KIDS (5437);
http://chicagochildrensbooks.com

MAGIC TREE
141 N. Oak Park Ave., Oak Park (708) 848-0770

WOMEN & CHILDREN FIRST
5233 N. Clark St., Chicago (773) 769-9299;
www.womenandchildrenfirst.com

To Market to Market
FARMERS' MARKETS

These days, Chicago and farming are rarely mentioned in the same sentence. But all summer long the two come together at farmers' markets across the city and the suburbs. Usually these festive, aromatic bazaars come to life every Saturday morning (other days in some locations). They're great places to bring kids and pick up tasty fresh fruits and vegetables, young potted plants and fragrant flowers. All goods are trucked in from farms outside Chicago and from surrounding states.

Some markets offer more than fresh produce. You can stock up on preserves and other prepared foods, hear musical performers, mingle with local residents and sometimes see arts and crafts displays. One well-known market is found at Daley Plaza in the Loop. It's a favorite place for office workers to shop for supper fixings. Another popular market, the Oak Park Farmers Market, features a Kids' Day in July where face painters, story tellers and other entertainers keep the kids amused. The Deerfield Farmer's Market in the northern suburbs is also a good place for kids. For a round up of other farmer's markets in the area, visit: www.ci.chi.il.us/ConsumerServices/farmersmarket.htm

DALEY PLAZA FARMERS MARKET
Near the corner of Washington and Clark streets, Chicago.

DEERFIELD FARMERS MARKET
Corner of Deerfield Rd. and York Ave., Deerfield
(847) 945-5000
www.deerfieldil.org/farmmkt/farmersmarket.html

OAK PARK FARMERS MARKET
Parking lot of Pilgrim Congregational Church, 460 Lake St.,
Oak Park (708) 383-6400, ext. 2337
www.oprf.com/farmersmarket

Kids on Ice
ICE SKATING

Nothing chases away the winter blues better than a few laps around an ice skating rink. Follow that with a cup of hot cocoa and you've got the ingredients for a fun outing for the family. Kids love the speed and smoothness of skating, even if they sometimes end up on the ice (make sure they wear proper fitting headgear). Ice skating is great exercise!

Many ice skating rinks around Chicago offer free admission. Most have skate rentals and refreshment stands. Skate on State, arguably Chicago's most famous rink, is a free outdoor skating surface operated by the city in the heart of the Loop. It has a large sheet of ice and heated changing stations for relief from the cold. On Saturday mornings, lessons for kids are offered at no charge. The outdoor rink on Navy Pier (next to the carousel) is popular with families as well. Though smaller than Skate on State, this rink is surrounded by attractions, such as the Chicago Children's Museum (page 17), that make it an outstanding destination. There's no admission and skate rentals are available.

For more skating action, the Chicago Park District (www.chicagoparkdistrict.com) operates a handful of outdoor rinks around the city. The Chicago area also boasts numerous indoor rinks. Several, such as the Northbrook Sports Center and the Rolling Meadows Ice Arena, operate year-round. These facilities offer snack bars, pro shops and changing rooms. For a comprehensive list of Chicago-area rinks, indoor and outdoor, visit www.chicagoice.com

NAVY PIER ICE SKATING RINK
Navy Pier, Chicago (312) 595-PIER (7437)
www.navypier.com

NORTHBROOK SPORTS CENTER
1730 Pfingsten Rd., Northbrook (847) 291-2980

ROLLING MEADOWS ICE ARENA
3900 Owl Dr., Rolling Meadows (847) 818-3210

SKATE ON STATE
Bounded by State, Randolph, Washington and Dearborn streets, Chicago
www.ci.chi.il.us/SpecialEvents/SkateonState.html

Places to PAINT YOUR OWN POTTERY

Pots, plates, mugs, statues . . . you name it, your kids can make them and paint them at one of the Chicago-area ceramic studios. Some of these studios feature already completed bisques (ceramic items) that simply need to be painted with non-toxic paints. The studio supplies the paint, brushes, stencils, sponges and tips to get your kids' creative juices rolling. Some studios charge by the hour in addition to the cost of the bisques, which start at about $5. Younger children tend to finish their projects quickly, so it's a good idea to put a limit on the number of items they can paint, or this activity will become expensive.

The shops have hundreds of different bisques and finished pieces that kids can look at for ideas. After the painting is done, the shop finishes the job by glazing and firing the piece. You can pick it up a few days later. Paint-your-own-pottery studios are great for crafty birthday parties!

Two popular shops, The Pot You Paint in Oak Park, and Color Me Mine with locations in Highland Park and Wheaton, offer this type of clean, artistic activity. For a studio near you, check the telephone book under "Ceramics." More serious potters might like taking a pottery class at a studio. One such place is The Pot Shop in Evanston. For the names of other studios offering pottery classes, contact your local park district and/or community arts center.

COLOR ME MINE
610 Central Ave., Highland Park (847) 266-1080
125 W. Front St., Wheaton (630) 665-1400
www.colormemine.com

THE POT SHOP
604 Dempster St., Evanston (847) 864-7778
www.potshop.com

THE POT YOU PAINT
121 N. Marion St., Oak Park (708) 660-1707
www.potyoupaint.com

Recreation Galore
PARK DISTRICTS

The Chicago-area park districts are undoubtedly the biggest source of affordable fun. They offer children's entertainment and recreation year-round. Park districts operate the pools, rinks, playgrounds and green spaces in their respective communities. But did you know they do even more? The Chicago Park District (312-742-7529; www.chicagoparkdistrict.com) for example, has hundreds of arts and crafts classes for children, countless special holiday events like Valentine's Day In the Park, and unlimited athletic opportunities for all tastes. One special program called Sports 37 is designed to provide kids with healthy activities such as intramural athletics and field trips for after school. Sports 37 even offers job training opportunities. Kids get the chance to do work as lifeguards, referees and coaches and gain valuable work experience. Suburban park districts offer kids similar activities on a smaller scale. Visit your local park district's website for information.

Since the park districts are subsidized, fees for classes and other activities are always easy on the family budget. And so much—like sledding, skating, walking, running or biking—is absolutely free!

Let the Children Play
PLAY LOTS

Want a sure-fire way to make your kids happy? Take them to a play lot. Few children can resist the lure. There's freedom to run, climb, slide, jump, dig, swing and more. Chicago and its suburbs are chock-full of play lots. Most Chicago Park District parks (www.chicagopark district.com) and suburban parks have them.

Some, like Cummings Playlot near the west gate of Lincoln Park Zoo (page 139) are quite elaborate. Kids' imaginations run wild as they try out its many slides, ladders, swings and sandboxes. An amazing wooden play complex is found at Indian Boundary Park on the North Side (page 137). One of the newest and most exciting playlots is at Priory Park in west suburban River Forest. This ultra-modern structure is a kid paradise! It features ladders, slides, a climb-on pirate ship, climbing nets and sandboxes. Best of all, these play lots are modern and safe, with many featuring rubberized surfaces and equipment designed to prevent dangerous falls.

CUMMINGS PLAYLOT
On Stockton Dr. south of Fullerton Ave., Chicago

INDIAN BOUNDARY PARK
2500 W. Lunt Ave., Chicago (312) 742-7887

PRIORY PARK
Division St. at Bonnie Brae St., River Forest
(708) 366-6660; www.rfpd.com

Cool Places to Play
SWIMMING POOLS

N othing's more refreshing on a hot, muggy midwestern afternoon than a dip in a cool pool with a couple hundred neighborhood kids! Community pools are Chicago's first lines of defense against the heat of summer. They do the job well. The Chicago Park District (312-742-7529; www.chicagoparkdistrict.com) operates 86 pools across the city—including 33 indoor pools open year-round. Nearly every suburb has one or more pools. Visit your local park district's website for their location and hours.

Some community pools are elaborate water parks. Others are more modest. Nearly all have changing rooms and snack bars, and lifeguards are always present. Many Chicago-area community pools are free to use. Some offer daily or seasonal passes.

CHAPTER 4

PLACES TO PLAY

Introduction

When your kids demand fun, Chicago offers plenty of options. Downtown, DisneyQuest features five floors of Disney-quality amusements and rides. ESPN Zone™, next door, is where sports lovers and others find an overwhelming variety of realistic sports simulators and virtual reality machines. For serious roller coaster fans, nothing beats visiting Six Flags Great America in Gurnee, which also has midway rides, shows and parades. If high-speed boating or go-karting is more your thing, look no further than Odyssey Fun World. There truly is a ride for everyone at Kiddieland, where 50-year-old carousel rides and miniature trains are located next to modern day thrills. Read on to learn about these attractions in more detail. The chapter also contains information on family arcades, wave pools, a skateboard park and more.

Skateboarders' Delight
BURNHAM SKATE PARK

34th St. and Lake Shore Dr., Chicago
(312) 742-PLAY (7529)
www.chicagoparkdistrict.com

S kateboarders and in-line skaters can whoop it up at Burnam Skate Park. This 20,000 square-foot area offers a safe environment, with separate challenges for advanced and novice skaters.

Pyramids and spines test skaters' skills. There are also benches, curbs and rails for performing all the tricks. The surface edges are capped with a smooth, curved metal facing to protect the skateboarders from concrete abrasions. Input from skaters was solicited when the park was in the planning stages.

Even if no one in your family skates, it's worth visiting the park just to watch the action—perhaps on your way to the 31st Street Beach. If you do plan to skate, remember to wear headgear, pads for your elbows and knees, and gloves.

SEASONS AND TIMES
➤ Mar—Oct: Mon—Fri, noon—6 pm; Sat—Sun, 10 am—6 pm.

COST
➤ Free.

GETTING THERE

➤ By car, take Lake Shore Dr. south to the 31st St. Exit. Look for parking along the beach. Walk south to the park. About 10 minutes from Grant Park.

NEARBY

➤ 31st St. Beach.

COMMENT

➤ The 31st St. Beach has beautiful views of downtown.

A *Taste of Make-believe*
DISNEYQUEST

55 E. Ohio St., Chicago
(312) 222-1300
www.disney.go.com/disneyquest

A blast of pure Disney magic awaits visitors at DisneyQuest in downtown Chicago. This large, indoor emporium features five floors of games, rides and other amusements overseen by professional, courteous "cast members."

Kids will make a beeline for the simulated rides—the park's most popular attractions. Height restrictions apply on some rides. In the Virtual Jungle Cruise, young adventurers visit Dinosaur Land in a rubber raft, twisting and bobbing down a river that is projected onto a screen. Watch out for the splashing water! For action-packed excitement head to Invasion! An Extra TERRORestial Alien Encounter. There you will use your weapon to fight off aliens while saving stranded colonists during a daring rescue mission. Aladdin's Magic Carpet Ride offers youngsters a virtual trip through the Cave of Wonders and other exciting places. At CyberSpace Mountain, you get to design your own roller coaster and ride it in a full 360-degree pitch-and-roll simulator.

DisneyQuest features tamer, more cerebral amusements as well. Magic Mirror gives budding photo artists the chance to manipulate images of themselves on computer screens. At Animation Academy, a trained artist shows youngsters the finer points of drawing cartoons. Simpler games—from air hockey to pinball machines to the latest in video games—round out the experience.

SEASONS AND TIMES
➤ Year-round: Sun—Wed, 11 am—7 pm; Thu—Fri, 11 am—10 pm; Sat, 10 am—10 pm.

COST
➤ Ultimate Play Game Card (unlimited play on all attractions and games): Adults $34, children (3 to 7) $26, under 3 free. Late night tickets sold 2 hours before closing, 50 % off.

GETTING THERE
➤ By car, take Michigan Ave. north to Ohio St. Turn west and travel 1 block. You will see DisneyQuest on the north side of the street. Pay parking in lots in the neighborhood. About 5 minutes from Grant Park.
➤ By public transit, take any CTA bus heading north on Michigan and get off at Ohio.

NEARBY
➤ ESPN Zone™, Water Tower, Hancock Center, Magnificent Mile.

COMMENT
➤ Have a problem? DisneyQuest's cast members will solve it quickly and efficiently. Plan a 3-hour visit.

Let the Games Begin
ENCHANTED CASTLE

1103 S. Main St., Lombard
(630) 953-7860
www.enchanted.com

I f your kids are into video games, they'll love Enchanted Castle. This king-size arcade has enough amusements to keep everyone occupied for hours.

The games are operated by tokens, and tickets will be dispensed after play is finished, depending on how well you did. Save those tickets. They can be redeemed for prizes—ranging from rubber bouncy balls to small appliances. Enchanted Castle's non-video amusements also have this feature. Kids can play skee ball, shoot water cannons, milk a life-size faux cow and more in pursuit of tickets.

There are other attractions. The younger set will flock to ImaGYMnation Station, an elaborate play area with tunnels, nets, slides and ball pits. They'll enjoy trying one of the ride-on vehicles (token-operated), such as the Batmobile or the bulldozer. Older visitors like the small bumper car arena, two-lane bowling alley and nine-hole miniature golf course. A laser tag arena and The Rage, a thrilling ride/movie combination, round out the fun.

Enchanted Castle is one of many arcade-type emporiums in the Chicago area. A sampling of others is listed under Restaurant Arcades on page 82.

SEASONS AND TIMES

➤ Year-round: Sun—Thu, 11 am—9 pm; Fri—Sat, 10 am—11 pm.

COST

➤ Games and amusements priced individually. Most games run on tokens that cost $0.25 each, or 24 for $5. Prices for other amusements vary. ImaGYMnation Station costs $4 per child (accompanying adults free) and miniature golf $3.

GETTING THERE

➤ By car, take I-290 W. to I-88 W. and continue on I-88 to the Roosevelt Rd. W. Exit. Travel west on Roosevelt to the corner of Roosevelt and Main St. in Lombard. Enchanted Castle is in the Lombard Pines Mall on the north side of Roosevelt. Free parking on site. About 45 minutes from Grant Park.

COMMENT

➤ Plan a 2-hour visit.

Faster, Higher, Stronger
ESPN ZONE™

43 E. Ohio St., Chicago
(312) 644-3776
www.espn.go.com/espninc/zone/index.html

ESPN Zone™ welcomes visitors to indulge their sports fantasies. This hi-tech recreational complex features simulated and virtual sports that run the gamut—from the conventional to the extreme. It's an ideal place to bring enthusiasts ages eight and up.

The most exciting attractions make you feel part of the action. Ever dreamed about jumping out of an airplane? You'll get your chance at the virtual reality sky diving machine. Divers strap on a chute complete with a rip cord and don a headset that provides all the visual cues of the fall. Prospective mountaineers scale the face of the rock-climbing machine. The climbing surface slowly rotates and makes reaching the summit next to impossible.

Basketball, hockey, alpine skiing and other sports are represented—in simulation of course. Each machine recreates the sensation of being in the play. There's no end to the amusements for speed lovers either. ESPN Zone™ has race games with realistic ride-on vehicles, including motorcycles and cars.

You'll find these games and simulated sports machines on the Zone's second floor. The ground floor houses a large family restaurant.

SEASONS AND TIMES
➤ Year-round: Mon—Thu, 11:30 am—midnight; Fri—Sat, 11:30 am—12:30 am; Sun, 11:30 am—11:30 pm.

COST
➤ Games are priced on a point basis, with games costing from 3 to 20 points. A 15-point debit card costs $6; a 40-point card $11 and a 100-point card $21.

GETTING THERE
➤ By car, take Michigan Ave. north to Ohio St. Turn east onto Ohio and travel 2 blocks. ESPN Zone™ is on the north side of the street. Parking available in pay lots in the neighborhood. About 5 minutes from Grant Park.
➤ By public transit, take any CTA bus heading north on Michigan and get off at Ohio.

NEARBY
➤ DisneyQuest, Water Tower, Hancock Center, Magnificent Mile.

COMMENT
➤ During certain times of the day, watch live ESPN radio broadcasts originating from the Zone through its glass-walled studio. Plan a 2-hour visit.

Nostalgic Fun
KIDDIELAND

North Ave. and First Ave., Melrose Park
(708) 343-8000
www.kiddieland.com

Kids love Kiddieland for its rides and amusements—many originating from the 1950s and earlier. You'll love Kiddieland for the happy childhood memories these rides evoke.

The reminiscing begins inside the gate with an old-time carousel featuring pint-sized bicycles, sports cars, fire engines, motorcycles and cable cars all spinning about. Kids ride these ancient vehicles with glee, oblivious to the nostalgia their grandparents and parents feel. The Kiddieland Express is a bona fide miniature steam engine locomotive in perfect working condition despite being decades old. It pulls a train of wooden and steel cars around the perimeter of the park. Adults ride too.

There is another carousel with horses and other tame, ride-on attractions, including space ships and boats, a Dumbo the Elephant ride and a mushroom spinning ride. Tots will be happiest digging in the large sand box.

Older kids aren't left out. A fantastic wooden roller coaster provides a gut-thumping thrill and a log ride splashes kids as it plunges along its path. Classic carnival rides such as Tilt-a-Whirl and the Galleon are sure bets for the 6- to 16-year-old set. Don't miss Kiddieland's newest addition, The Drop. It sets your equilibrium askew as it bounces up and down.

SEASONS AND TIMES
➤ Mid-Apr—late Oct. Schedule varies by the month. Call for dates and times or visit the website.

COST
➤ Individuals (6 and up) $17.50, children (3 to 5) $14.50, under 3 free. After 5 pm $3 off each admission.

GETTING THERE
➤ By car, take I-290 W. to the First Ave. Exit. Drive north on First to North Ave. Kiddieland is on the northwest corner. Free parking on site. About 30 minutes from Grant Park.

NEARBY
➤ Cernan Space and Earth Center, Hal Tyrell Trailside Museum.

COMMENT
➤ Kiddieland has rides for young children and teens and is perfect for families with children of mixed ages. Plan a 3-hour visit.

High-flying Fun
KIDS ON THE FLY

O'Hare Airport, Terminal 2, Chicago
(312) 527-1000

Kids on the Fly is a real life-saver for families stranded at O'Hare Airport. Kids can live out their pilot fantasies in this play area while waiting for the real plane to take off. If you've brought your children to O'Hare to see how an airport operates, this is a good place for them to blow off steam.

Designed by the Chicago Children's Museum, the play area is entirely fenced and has benches where parents can take in the action. In the center is a giant mock up of an airplane. The highlight is the cockpit. It can accommodate up to four kids who crank its steering wheels, dials and knobs and talk over the telephone to other kids in the tower. A cargo hold at the rear of the plane has giant toy boxes that can be loaded and off loaded.

The tower is the next most popular attraction. There, older travelers get a quick lesson in meteorology, while littler tykes are happy to be high up talking to the pilot on the telephone. A luggage handling area and a crate maze round out the set up.

SEASONS AND TIMES
➼ Open when airport is open.

COST
➤ Free, but officially for ticketed passengers only.

GETTING THERE
➤ By car, take I-90 W. to I-190 W. and follow to the airport. The play area is located in Terminal 2. Pay parking on site. About 40 minutes from Grant Park.

➤ By public transit, take the Blue line El (a subway in the Loop) to O'Hare at one of three underground stations on Dearborn St.

COMMENT
➤ The playthings are large enough that adults can join their children.

Full-speed Ahead for
ODYSSEY FUN WORLD

19111 S. Oak Park Ave., Tinley Park
(708) 429-3800
www.odysseyfunworld.com

O dyssey Fun World, an indoor-outdoor amusement center, is overflowing with high-speed, high-energy fun.

Outside, older kids get a kick out of Snake Water Island, where they maneuver bumper boats through giant, hissing monster jaws and dodge the 15-foot geyser. Hydro Racer Speed Boats put them in the drivers' seats of small, speedy boats they race on a quarter-mile track. Two go-kart tracks, nine batting cages (for baseball or softball) and two 18-hole miniature golf courses that take players through a mine shaft and around a Mayan temple, complete the set-up for big kids.

There are lots of rides for younger kids, too. The KIDZ Adventure Park, designed for those 12 and under, features a bumper boat pond, a Ferris wheel, the Odyssey Fun World Express Train and other pint-sized delights.

Indoors, over 250 arcade and video games will keep your kids' eyes aglaze. The MaxFlight VR 2002 roller coaster simulator offers thrill-seekers an exciting ride without the wind in their faces. Tots won't want to leave Exploration Adventure where they can climb, slide and swim in a pool of colorful balls.

SEASONS AND TIMES
➤ Summer (June—Aug): Daily, indoor, 10 am—midnight; outdoor, 11 am—11 pm. Winter (Sept—May): Indoors only; Sun—Thu, 10 am—10 pm; Fri—Sat, 10 am—midnight.

COST
➤ Amusements priced individually. Bumper boats, go-karts and similar rides: $6 per ride. KIDZ Adventure Park: Four rides for $6. Exploration Adventure: $5.95 per person. Video game tokens: $0.25 each, or 100 for $20.

GETTING THERE
➤ By car, take I-90/94 E. to I-57 S. Go south on I-57 until I-80 and take it west to Harlem Ave. S. Exit. Follow Harlem south until Oak Park Ave. Turn east and continue on to Odyssey Fun World. Free parking on site. About 45 minutes from Grant Park.

COMMENT
➤ Plan a 3-hour visit.

Avast Ye Buccaneers!
PIRATE'S COVE

**Leicester Rd. and Biesterfield Rd., Elk Grove Village
(847) 437-9494
www.elkgrove.org/egpd/Pages/PiratesCove.html**

The next time your kids say "Let's play pirates," take them to Pirate's Cove. This outdoor theme park, run by the Elk Grove Village Park District, has amusements with a pirate theme that kids love.

The Castle of Camelot features a maze of tunnels, nets, tires and tubes that will stimulate your little buccaneers' imaginations as they get a work out. Nearby, Smuggler's Crag is a 20-foot-high climbing wall that accommodates various skill levels. An authentic-looking pirate ship offers families a place to play make-believe and picnic. The Pirate Town Gate House serves as the park's field house. It has washrooms, drinking fountains and a souvenir shop.

Landlubbers enjoy the Old Fashioned Carousel and the Eureka Train Ride that travels through a tunnel and past the old Eureka Mine. Don't forget the Jungle Cruise Ride with its gaggle of friendly animals, or the Bumper Boats where kids can bump and splash their friends.

Pirate's Cove is a popular place for birthday parties. Packages are available and reservations are required.

SEASONS AND TIMES
➤ June 11—Aug 17: Mon—Wed, 11 am—5 pm and 6 pm—8 pm; Thu—
Fri, 11 am—5 pm; Sat, 10 am—4 pm; Sun, noon—4 pm.

COST
➤ Adults free, children $6 ($1 discount for Elk Grove residents). $2
off Mon—Wed evenings. $1 off Sundays.

GETTING THERE
➤ By car, take I-290 W. to the Biesterfield Rd. Exit. Drive east on
Biesterfield 1/2 mile to Leicester Rd. and turn south. There's parking
just south of the intersection. About 40 minutes from Grant Park.

NEARBY
➤ Rainbow Falls, O'Hare Airport.

COMMENT
➤ Plan a 2-hour visit.

Take the Plunge
RAINBOW FALLS
WATER PARK

**Corner of Lions Dr. and Elk Grove Blvd.,
Elk Grove Village
(847) 228-2890
www.elkgrove.org/egpd/Pages/RainbowFalls.html**

Keeping cool during the balmy Chicago
summer is a lot more fun since water parks
began operating. Rainbow Falls Water Park

is very popular and entertains visitors with over five acres of slides, pools and other watery toys.

Everyone enjoys getting soaked in the Fun-House. This three-story amusement is full of interactive water "gags" that spray, splash and wet down swimmers as they clamber through. Reach the top and ride an 80-foot enclosed tube slide back to the pool. (Parents can accompany younger children who are too afraid to slide solo.) Some rides have height restrictions, such as the three Water Flume Slides. Big kids love the thrill of racing down these slides with all their twists and turns. Only the bravest attempt the 300-foot Tube Ride. It leaves riders gasping for air.

The Junior Waterslide and Adventure Pool is a special area Rainbow Falls has set aside for its littler patrons. Kids too young to enjoy the large slides can shoot each other with water cannons, climb through dripping wet tunnels and pretend to be Tarzan while swinging across the Adventure Pool. The Wading Pool is perfect for toddlers who are just getting used to water.

SEASONS AND TIMES
➤ Memorial Day—Labor Day Weekend: Mon—Fri, 10 am—7 pm; Sat—Sun, 10 am—5 pm.

COST
➤ Individuals $9, children (2 to 5) $8, under 2 free. Elk Grove residents $6.

GETTING THERE
➤ By car, take I-290 W. to the Biesterfield Rd. Exit. Travel east on Biesterfield through downtown Elk Grove Village until Biesterfield

ends at Elk Grove Blvd. Turn north on Elk Grove and drive to Lions Dr. Turn west onto Lions. Rainbow Falls is behind the Elk Grove High School. Free parking on site. About 40 minutes from Grant Park.

NEARBY
➤ Pirate's Cove, O'Hare Airport.

COMMENT
➤ Pack sun screen and hats as the pool area is fully exposed to the sun. Qualified lifeguards staff the park. Dry off after your swim and play miniature golf at the Rainbow Falls' course. Plan a 2-hour visit.

Other Family Water Parks

Wheeling Aquatic Center and Arctic Splash
327–333 W. Dundee Rd., Wheeling
(847) 465-3333
www.wheelingparkdistrict.com/aquaticcenter.html

The Wheeling Aquatic Center is a blast of fun on hot summer days. It features a tube slide, two drop slides and Willie the Whale Toddler Slide. There is a sandy play area and a playground. On the same site, Arctic Splash is an indoor pool offering water play structures, a toddler slide and a whirlpool.

➤ Aquatic Center: Early June—early Sept, Mon—Fri, noon—9 pm; Sat—Sun, 11 am—7 pm. Arctic Splash: Year-round, hours vary.

➤ Aquatic Center: Individuals (3 and over) $9, under 3 free. Half price after 5 pm. Arctic Splash: Individuals (2 and over) $6, under 2 free.

➤ Take I-90 W. to I-294 W./N. Travel on I-294 to the Willow Rd. Exit. Go west on Willow to Milwaukee Ave. and turn north to Dundee Rd. Turn west on Dundee and take it to Northgate Pkwy. Turn south on Northgate and follow the curve to the free parking lot. Arctic Splash is inside the Community Recreation Center. The Aquatic Center is beside it.

Seascape Family Aquatic Center
1300 Moon Lake Blvd., Hoffman Estates
(847) 781-2399
www.nsn.org/sckhome/heparks/ssc.html

The Seascape Family Aquatic Center has body flumes, tube slides, diving boards, drop slides, lap lanes, a water playground and other fun-in-the-water features.

➤ Memorial Day—Labor Day (weekends only until mid-June); Mon—Fri, 11:30 am—8:30 pm; Sat—Sun, 11 am—8 pm.

➤ Adults $8, youths (4 to 17) $6, under 4 free.

➤ Take I-90 west to the Barrington Rd. Exit. Go south on Barrington to Higgins Rd. Turn east and take Higgins to Moon Lake Blvd. Turn south on Moon Lake. The center is on the west side.

WaterWorks
505 Springinsguth Rd., Schaumburg
(847) 490-7020

WaterWorks is an indoor water park that features an array of fun slides, including a drop slide. There are also diving boards and a sandy play area for kids.

➤ Year-round: Hours and days vary. Call for times.

➤ Adults $8, youths (3 to 17) $6, under 3 free.

➤ Take I-290 west to the Higgins Rd. Exit. Travel west on Higgins to Meacham Rd. Turn south following Meacham to Schaumburg Rd. Turn west on Schaumburg to Springinsguth Rd. Follow Springinsguth north to WaterWorks.

Chicago Park District
(312) 742-PLAY (7529)
www.chicagoparkdistrict.com

Chicago residents can now enjoy interactive water parks in their own community. Recently, the Chicago Park District built four new parks. Each comes equipped with waterslides, tunnels, pipes, spraying equipment and other cool and refreshing amenities. You'll find them at Foster Park (1440 W. 84th St.), LaFollette Park (1333 N. Laramie Ave.), Riis Park (6100 W. Fullerton Ave.) and West Chatham Park (8223 S. Princeton Ave.).

➤ Memorial Day—Labor Day: Mon—Fri, 9 am—8 pm; Sat—Sun, 9:30 am—8 pm.

➤ Free.

Fun and Food
RESTAURANT ARCADES
Jeepers
www.jeepers.com

Jeepers is a national chain of popular restaurants/ indoor amusement parks featuring five or six pint-sized rides. There's no end to the fun youngsters have on the Python Pit roller coaster, JJ's Driving School mini bumper cars and other attractions. In addition, the parks feature play areas with tubes, chute slides, obstacle courses and arcade-type games such as Hungry Hippos and basketball hoop shoots. Players can earn tickets playing the games and redeem them later for trinkets. Little wonder Jeepers is a popular birthday party place; make your reservations today.

723 Golf Rd., Des Plaines • (847) 640-6099
91 E. North Ave., Glendale Heights • (630) 510-7000
4516 N. Harlem Ave., Norridge • (708) 452-8800

Chuck E. Cheese
www.chuckecheese.com

Chuck E. Cheese, another national chain of arcade/ restaurant complexes, features pizza along with musical robotic animals and lots of games for kids. Youngsters enjoy the play area complete with tunnels, slides and a ball pit. Older kids like the video games, skee ball and other, more sophisticated amusements. Keep the tickets dispensed, they can be exchanged for goodies at the end. Everyone enjoys the antics of Chuckie and his gang of animatronic pals who sing songs and entertain diners. Chuck E. Cheese is a popular venue for kids' birthday parties; make your reservations early.

1730 W. Fullerton Ave., Chicago • (773) 871-2484
5080 S. Kedzie, Chicago • (773) 476-0500
511 N. Randall Rd., Batavia • (630) 482-2402
7409 Casa St., Darien • (630) 964-0740
1314 North Ave., Melrose Park • (708) 343-1224
1154 E. Ogden, Naperville • (630) 369-2012
7142 Carpenter Rd., Skokie • (847) 679-8180

Big Park Thrills
SIX FLAGS GREAT AMERICA

542 N. Rt. 21, Gurnee
(847) 249-4636
www.sixflags.com/greatamerica

For the total amusement park experience, nothing compares to Six Flags Great America. From giant roller coasters to dazzling stage shows, this is the real thing.

No fewer than seven roller coasters will send your older children flying, spinning, whipping and dropping at amazing speeds. The biggest is Raging Bull, accelerating to 73 miles per hour with a first drop of 200 feet. Those daring enough to try Batman: The Ride, hang off the bottom of the track as the coaster performs drops and loops at 50 miles per hour. The Iron Wolf whips riders who are standing through a corkscrew loop, hairpin turns and a 90-foot drop.

Great America hasn't forgotten the younger set. Endless hours of fun await them at Looney Tunes National Park. Among its attractions are Looney Tunes Lodge where kids frolic amid thousands of foam balls, and Pepe Lepew's Peak, a climbing and sliding complex. Camp Cartoon Network, another kid favorite, has pint-sized rides. Spacely's Sprocket Rockets, Yogi Bear's Yahoo River Boat Ride and the junior roller coaster are the most popular.

In between rides, check out the stage show. In the past, Great America has entertained crowds with *Great Russian Circus* and *American Rock!* Parades are featured and costumed characters roam the park ready to entertain your kids.

SEASONS AND TIMES

➤ Mid-May—late May: Mon—Fri, 10 am—6 pm; Sat—Sun, 10 am—9 pm. Early June—mid-June: Daily, 10 am—9 pm. Mid-June—Aug: Daily, 10 am—10 pm. Sept: Sat—Sun, 10 am—8 pm. Oct: Fri, 5 pm—11 pm; Sat, 10 am—9 pm; Sun, 10 am—8 pm.

COST

➤ Adults $42.99, children (under 48 inches) $21.49, under 2 free.

GETTING THERE

➤ By car, take I-94 W. to the Grand Ave. Exit (Rt. 132) East. You'll see Six Flags immediately on your right. Pay parking on site ($8). About 1 hour from Grant Park.

COMMENT

➤ Plan an all-day visit.

CHAPTER 5

PLACES
TO LEARN

Introduction

F or kids, learning doesn't have to be a dull experience. Lots of places in the Chicago area that feature exciting educational opportunities make sure fun is part of the outing. In fact, kids won't realize they are learning when they visit two outstanding children's museums in Wilmette and Wheaton. The DuPage Children's Museum and the Kohl Children's Museum are packed with activities and interactive exhibits to stimulate little minds. Imaginations can reach for the stars at Adler Planetarium and Cernan Space and Earth Center. For pure and applied science fun, check out the array of hands-on experiments at SciTech Interactive Science Center.

There's more excitement at JFK Health World, where youngsters come away with a better understanding about their bodies and think they were at an amusement park when it happened. Read about these places in this chapter and find out about others where kids can immerse themselves in art and history, experience campus life at one of Chicago's fine universities, see how chocolates are made and more.

A *Celestial Show* at the
ALDER PLANETARIUM &
ASTRONOMY MUSEUM

1300 S. Lake Shore Dr., Chicago
(312) 322-0304
www.adlerplanetarium.org

If your kids sometimes seem like they have their heads in the clouds, take them to Adler Planetarium to experience the world beyond. The highlight of your trip just may be the StarRider Theater. It uses computer projection technology to present 3-D, interactive shows such as *Blueprint for a Red Planet*—a simulated space flight to Mars. More space exploration is found at the Zeiss Sky Show Theater, where a special projector displays the stars, planets and constellations on a domed ceiling.

Adler has lots for kids after they see a show. They can operate a mini space rover by remote control, see themselves stretched out in mirrors that help to explain the phenomena of black holes, or take a short ride into the Atwood Sphere. It uses pinholes of light to depict what Chicago's night sky looked like when the Sphere was built in 1913. Astronomical history is also displayed at Adler, with exhibits of artifacts from ancient times to current NASA space trips.

One of the most enjoyable things about your visit to Adler is seeing the incredible view of the city thorough the planetarium's glass walls!

SEASONS AND TIMES
➤ Year-round, Mon—Thu, 9 am—5 pm; Fri, 9 am—9 pm; Sat—Sun, 9 am—6 pm.

COST
➤ Adults $5, children (4 to 17) $4, under 4 free. Show tickets an additional $5 per person.

GETTING THERE
➤ By car, take Columbus Dr. south to McFetridge Dr. Turn east onto the Museum Campus and follow McFetridge until it curves onto Solidarity Dr. Adler is at the very end of the peninsula. Park in the museum's pay lot ($7), or on the street. About 5 minutes from Grant Park.

➤ By public transit, take CTA bus 6 (Jeffrey Express) on State St. to the corner of Roosevelt Rd. and Columbus Dr. In the summer, a free trolley service runs from various downtown locations to the Museum Campus.

NEARBY
➤ Field Museum, Shedd Aquarium, 12th St. Beach.

COMMENT
➤ Dining in Galileo's Café is a pleasant experience, mixing quality food with unmatched views of the lake and Chicago skyline. Plan at least a 2-hour visit.

Seeing Stars
CERNAN EARTH AND SPACE CENTER

Triton College, 2000 Fifth Ave., River Grove
(708) 583-3100
www.triton.cc.il.us/cernan/cernan_home.html

Kids' imaginations soar at the Cernan Earth and Space Center. The highlight for everyone is the Center's 100-seat theater, where laser light spectaculars and kids' movies about space are projected onto a domed ceiling. Comfortable reclining chairs give the audience the sensation of floating in space.

The museum at the Center is small, but its genuine space travel exhibits pack a punch. Astronaut Eugene Cernan's space suit is among the displays. He was the last man to visit the moon and is the Center's namesake. You will also see the gloves that astronaut Harrison Schmitt wore when he walked on the moon and rocket engines that powered various space missions. Don't miss the lunar module, which the U.S. Navy used as a trainer for ocean recoveries, and the Tomahawk missile that dominate the museum entrance.

The museum has a few interactive exhibits that will fascinate kids. Among them is Moon Shadows where visitors can manipulate the moon's position and observe its changing phases. A two-part diorama, one depicting the moon during the Apollo landings and the other the surface of Mars, make for interesting viewing. The Doppler Weather Radar exhibit lets children follow actual storms crossing the Midwest. The museum's Earth exhibit has a broad collection of Illinois fossils and a model of a dinosaur footprint that kids like to ogle.

SEASONS AND TIMES
➤ Year-round: Mon—Thu, 9 am—5 pm; Fri, 9 am—11 pm; Sat, 1 pm—11 pm; Sun, 1 pm—5 pm. Closed major holidays.

COST
➤ Earth and Sky Show: Adults $5, children (12 and under) $2.50. Laser Light Show: Adults $7, children (12 and under) $3.50. Admission to the museum is free.

GETTING THERE
➤ By car, take I-290 west to the First Ave. Exit. Travel north on First to North Ave. Turn west and drive to Fifth Ave. Turn north on Fifth and you will see the campus straddling the road. Turn in at the college main entrance (on the west side of Fifth) and travel to Cernan's building at the north end of the campus. Free parking on site. About 45 minutes from Grant Park.

NEARBY
➤ Kiddieland, Frank Lloyd Wright Home and Studio.

COMMENT
➤ Allow 30 minutes for the museum and an hour for a show.

Building Smarter Kids
DUPAGE CHILDREN'S MUSEUM

301 N. Washington St., Naperville
(630) 260-9960
www.dcmrats.org

Young visitors will have a blast learning about science and other subjects while exploring this museum's interactive exhibits. It is the quintessential hands-on place!

The action starts in the Construction House where children can use real adult tools such as hammers and saws (under close adult supervision) to make take-home projects out of scrap materials. Eye protection is provided and must be worn at all times. The next exciting stop is AirWorks for Kids, a fascinating exhibit with displays that demonstrate the characteristics of moving air. Youngsters can float balls on air columns and insert streamers into a maze of transparent air tubes. In Ramps & Rollers, up-and-coming engineers create pathways for balls using wooden blocks and inclines. The Kid-Netic Motion Machine requires kids to use their bodies to power a ball down a musical path.

Waterworks is another popular station. It features dams and waterwheels that youngsters can operate to control the flow of water along an 88-foot-long stream. Also on the "must see" list is Giant Pin Screen which creates 3-D imprints of whatever body part touches it.

Throughout the museum you will see children in wheelchairs. Most are trying them out to experience life for the physically disabled.

SEASONS AND TIMES
➤ Year-round: Mon (open to members only), 9 am—noon; Tue, 9:30 am—5 pm; Wed, 9:30 am—8 pm; Thu—Sat, 9:30 am—5 pm; Sun, noon—5 pm.

COST
➤ Adults and children (1 and up) $4.50, under 1 free.

GETTING THERE
➤ Take I-290 west to I-88. Travel west on I-88 to the Naperville Rd. Exit. Turn south on Naperville until Ogden Ave. and head west to Washington St. Turn south and drive to the museum. Free parking on site. About 1 hour from Grant Park.

NEARBY
➤ Morton Arboretum, Willowbrook Wildlife Center.

COMMENT
➤ Plan a 2-hour visit.

SIMILAR ATTRACTION
➤ **Oak Park Children's Museum.** A popular attraction for west suburban families. Displays on architecture, sound and hearing, an interactive theater and other stimulating features are among the planned exhibits. 6445 North Ave., Oak Park. (The museum's telephone number and website address were unavailable at press time.)

Healthy Fun
JFK HEALTH WORLD

1301 S. Grove Ave., Barrington
(847) 842-9100
www.healthworldmuseum.org

J FK Health World is an exceptionally entertaining romp through the world of human health. A gigantic, two-story model of a girl inside the entrance is a good sign of what awaits. Visitors can step inside the model's body for an up close look at the enormous heart and other organs. Inside the brain, a small theater has a short, interactive movie on the workings of the human mind. After the film kids will be eager to check out the scores of other fascinating hands-on stations.

The adventure continues at Dark Crawl, a display about sight. Children have to "feel" their way through a maze in complete darkness. Next they can test their reflexes on a computerized TV screen while pretending they are hockey goalies blocking shots. Similar technology at the ambulance and doctor's office exhibits put kids right in the action during medical emergencies.

The museum has even more. Youngsters can try out wheelchairs, watch themselves magically age on a computer screen, play an anti-smoking video game and make crafts from recycled products. In fact, JFK Health World has so many exhibits, you may want to save some of them for another visit.

SEASONS AND TIMES
➤ Year-round: Sat—Thu, 10 am—3 pm; Fri, 10 am—8 pm. Closed on major holidays and for 10 days each year at the beginning of September.

COST
➤ Adults and children $5, under 2 free.

GETTING THERE
➤ By car, take I-90/94 west to I-90 and continue traveling west to the Barrington Rd. Exit. Travel north on Barrington to Dundee Rd. Turn east on Dundee and drive about 1/2 mile to Grove Ave. Turn north on Grove. You will see the museum's green glass walls on the east side of the street. Free parking on site. About 1 hour from Grant Park.

COMMENT
➤ Plan a 2- to 3-hour visit.

Hands-on Learning
KOHL CHILDREN'S MUSEUM

165 Green Bay Rd., Wilmette
(847) 256-6056
www.kohlchildrensmuseum.org

"**L**earning by doing" is the philosophy of Kohl's Children's Museum. To accomplish this the museum provides scores of hands-on activities for kids.

Begin your visit at the Great Kohl Sailing Ship that lets junior mariners pretend they are sea captains crossing the ocean, or fishermen hauling in nets full of cloth fish. Their sea journey over, steer youngsters to the Construction Zone to install cushy wall panels and felt shingles on a large frame house. They will love operating the pulley lift beside the house (it only works if two children cooperate) and the crane that moves pillows that look like rocks.

The pace—not the fun—slows down in the museum's miniature grocery store. It features pint-size shopping carts with play groceries, baked goods and deli items. After filling their order, youngsters take their purchases to the checkout area, which has cash registers and scanners that beep. Others enjoy donning mini uniforms and pretending they are grocery store employees.

More fun awaits in the museum's other areas, including the H_2O room where kids can splish and splash while learning about water. The Motorola StarMax Technology Center has the latest in educational computer games and Grandma's Attic features a crawl-through maze that's chock-full of toys from two generations ago.

SEASONS AND TIMES
➤ Labor Day–June: Mon, 9 am–noon; Tue–Sat, 9 am–5 pm; Sun, noon–5 pm.

COST
➤ Adults and children (1 and up) $5, under 1 free.

GETTING THERE
➤ By car, take I-90/94 west to the Edens Expy. (I-94 N.) Go north on I-94 to the Lake Ave. E. Exit and head east on Lake to Green Bay Rd. Turn south and drive for about 5 blocks. The museum is on the west side of the street. There is free lot parking beside the museum. About 30 minutes from Grant Park

NEARBY
➤ Chicago Botanic Gardens.

COMMENT
➤ Listen for the public address announcements regarding supervised
art projects at the rear of Grandma's Attic. Plan at least a 2-hour visit.

Riding through History
LAKE COUNTY
DISCOVERY MUSEUM

Rte. 176 at Fairfield Rd., Wauconda
(847) 968-3400
www.co.lake.il.us/forest/educate.htm

For a roller coaster ride without that queasy
feeling, try the Vortex Roller Coaster Theater at
Lake County Discovery Museum. Three large
screens combine the visual cues of being on a speedy
coaster with a blast through millennia of Lake County
history. Vibrating seats add to its authenticity.

The coaster is one of many kid-friendly attractions at the museum, which takes a hands-on
approach to revealing this suburban northwest
county's past. Pick up a "Concept Card" at the main
desk. Kids love sliding them into the slots to activate
the exhibits. Slide the card into the display on 19th
century residents and you will hear the tale of four
individuals from that era. Slide it into a display on
local businesses and hear about important manu-
facturers that sprang up in the area.

Round everyone up for a boat ride—simulated of course—on the historic Lotus Cruise Line, which once plied local waterways. Youngsters love sitting in the small boat and following the action on the screen in front. Save some time to see the museum's collection of fossils and bones. Kids are permitted to touch the displays. Want to send an e-mail postcard to a friend back home? A separate gallery houses a vast postcard collection and an on-line postcard archive.

SEASONS AND TIMES
➤ Year-round: Mon—Sat, 11 am—4:30 pm; Sun, 1 pm—4:30 pm. Closed major holidays.

COST
➤ Adults $5, children (4 to 17) $2.50, under 4 free. Reduced admission on Tuesday: Adults $2.50, children (17 and under) free.

GETTING THERE
➤ By car, take I-90/94 west to I-90 west/north. Continue going north on I-90 (it becomes Rte. 41) until the Rte. 176 Exit. Travel west on Rte. 176 through the towns of Mundelein and Libertyville. About 100 yards past the intersection of 176 and Fairfield Rd., look for the entrance to Lakewood Forest Preserve on the south side of the road. Turn into the preserve and follow the signs to the museum. Free parking on site. About 50 minutes from Grant Park.

NEARBY
➤ Chicago Botanic Gardens.

COMMENT
➤ Pack a picnic. The forest preserve surrounding the museum is an excellent place for lunching. Plan a 90-minute visit.

The Art is the Draw
MEXICAN FINE ARTS CENTER MUSEUM

1852 W. 19th St., Chicago
(312) 738-1503
www.mfacmchicago.org

Beautiful art and exotic culture tastefully mingle in this small museum in Pilsen, a predominantly Mexican-American neighborhood in Chicago. Although the visit appeals to school-age children more than their younger siblings, some of the museum's exhibits will interest small children.

The museum maintains a permanent collection, currently numbering 2,400 paintings, photographs, sculptures and other artistic pieces. It features these and loaned items in a continually changing series of stimulating exhibitions that showcase the broad range of Mexican art. Recent exhibitions have included *Dia de Muertos* (*Day of the Dead*), an emotional, thought-provoking display of altars, paintings, sculptures and other objects honoring Mexico's day of remembering deceased friends and family; and *Americanos: Latin Life in the United States*, a collection of 120 photos of Latin-Americans at work and play.

The center offers more than static displays. It has guided tours and stages two performing arts festivals each year featuring concerts, dance productions, film screenings and other attractions. Educational programming is available for all ages, in the way of hands-on art-making activities. If your older children are interested in learning about radio, they might like Radio Arte. This youth-operated radio station at the center broadcasts to the Pilsen neighborhood and prepares 15- to 21-year-olds for careers in broadcast communications.

SEASONS AND TIMES
➤ Year-round: Tue—Sun, 10 am—5 pm.

COST
➤ Free.

GETTING THERE
➤ By car, take I-290 west to the Ashland Ave. Exit. Travel south on Ashland to 19th St. Take 19th west to the museum located in Harrison Park. Look for street parking (free). About 15 minutes from Grant Park.

COMMENT
➤ Notice that many of the houses across the street from the museum have front doors 6 to 10 feet below the street grade. This is a vivid remnant of a massive project the city undertook 150 years ago to improve drainage by raising city streets. Some homeowners could not afford to raise their houses, so they remained "sunken." Plan a 1-hour visit.

Science 101
SCITECH INTERACTIVE SCIENCE CENTER

18 W. Benton St., Aurora
(630) 859-3434
www.scitech.mus.il.us

C an a butterfly start a hurricane? Get the answer to that question and many others at SciTech (by the way, if you answered yes, you are correct). This gigantic science fair is packed with over 200 hands-on experiments situated on two floors and in the yard outside. SciTech really does have exhibits for all ages, from the elementary (push a button to fill a balloon with hot air so it rises to the ceiling) to the college-level.

One of the most popular displays is the tornado machine that lets kids put their hands in the middle of a funnel cloud. They can measure the speed of their fast ball at the pitching booth and dip gigantic "wands" into liquid soap to learn the physics behind bubble blowing. Even activities intended for older kids are fun for tykes, such as video games that demonstrate matter as they blast away at alien invaders. Younger children will most enjoy visiting the pre-schoolers' room in the basement. Here they can race balls down two inclined tracks (with surprising results), play with big, soft building blocks and more.

Every experiment in SciTech has easy-to-follow instructions and explanations about the science involved. Friendly staff are on hand should you need assistance.

SEASONS AND TIMES
➤ Year-round: Tue—Wed, noon—5 pm; Thu, noon—8 pm; Fri, noon—5 pm; Sat, 10 am—5 pm. Closed most major holidays.

COST
➤ Adults and children (2 and up) $5, families (up to 6 members, immediate family only) $15.

GETTING THERE
➤ By car, take I-290 west to I-88. Go west on I-88 to the Rte. 31 (Lake St.) Exit. Take Lake St. south to downtown Aurora. Turn east on Benton St. The museum is on the south side of Benton. There is metered street parking, or drive 1/2 block east of museum to Stolp Ave. Turn north and park at the Stolp Garage. Bring your parking receipt to the museum and they will validate it. About 1 hour from Grant Park.

NEARBY
➤ Morton Arboretum, Willowbrook Wildlife Center.

COMMENT
➤ SciTech's gift store is full of scientific games and toys. Plan a 2-hour visit.

Junior Ivy Leaguers
UNIVERSITY VISITS

C hicago is filled with institutions of higher learning. More than "schools," their campuses feature beautiful architecture, well-kept grounds, entertainment, museums, galleries and lots of young, energetic people. Visiting one can be a fun family trip. If any of your children are within a few years of graduating from high school, touring the campuses gives them a firsthand look at university life.

Below is information on three of Chicago's most prestigious universities. Before heading out to one, visit its website or call for the dates and times of upcoming concerts, theater performances or other cultural events. You can stroll through the campuses year-round.

University of Chicago
Hyde Park Neighborhood, Chicago
(773) 702-1234
www.uchicago.edu

Since John D. Rockefeller founded this prestigious university in 1891, its faculty and students have been awarded 72 Nobel Prizes—a key indicator of the quality of the education. Perhaps more interesting to visiting families is the awesome gothic architecture of many of the buildings that are arranged around a series of tree-shaded quadrangles. The most prominent building is Rockefeller Memorial Chapel with its 207-foot tower. The U of Chicago has cultural treasures on its enormous campus stretching along both sides of the grassy Midway Plaisance. Among them, the Oriental Institute Museum, the Court Theatre and the David and Alfred Smart Museum of Art.

➤ Take Lake Shore Dr. south until the 57th St. Exit. Follow 57th west as it curves around the Museum of Science and Industry and turn into Cornell Dr. heading south. Take Cornell to 59th St. Turn west and you will be on the north side of Midway Plaisance. Rockefeller Memorial Chapel is on the corner of 59th and Woodlawn St. There is limited street parking. About 15 minutes from Grant Park.

DePaul University
Lincoln Park Neighborhood, Chicago
(312) 362-8000
www.depaul.edu

DePaul, America's largest Catholic university, was founded in 1898 by the Vincentian Fathers to teach the children of immigrants. The university has six campuses in the Chicago area, but the main campus in Lincoln Park is the most interesting. Featuring 36 acres, it boasts a mix of modern and classical buildings with a grassy, shaded quadrangle in the middle. The university sponsors numerous public events throughout its year, including performances by students in the Theatre School and the School of Music.

➤ Take Lake Shore Dr. north to the Fullerton Ave. Exit. Travel west on Fullerton for about 3 miles to the campus, which is at the corner of Fullerton and Kenmore Ave. Street parking is available. About 15 minutes from Grant Park. Take the El (Brown or Red lines) to Fullerton stop. The campus is immediately south of the station.

Northwestern University
Evanston
(847) 491-3741
www.northwestern.edu

Founded in 1851, Northwestern University features a picturesque campus in north suburban Evanston that stretches for almost a mile along the shore of Lake Michigan. Visitors see a mix of historic and modern buildings set among beautifully land-scaped yards and quads that are perfect for strolling and people-watching. The campus features two art galleries, four venues for dance and theater performances and the Pick-Staiger Concert Hall, where events are scheduled all the time.

➻ Take Lake Shore Dr. north until it curves west and becomes Hollywood Ave. Travel west on Hollywood to Sheridan Rd. Go north on Sheridan for about 4 miles to the campus. Street parking and some lot parking available. About 25 minutes from Grant Park.
By public transit, take the Red line El to Howard stop. Transfer to Purple line El, and continue to Foster Ave. stop. Walk east for 3 blocks on Foster to the campus.

Other Places to Learn

Goelitz Confectionery Company

1539 Morrow Ave., North Chicago
(847) 689-8950
www.jellybelly.com/newhome/tour_chicago.html

If you've ever dreamed of visiting a real candy factory, here's your chance. The Goelitz Confectionery Company, which makes jelly beans, chocolates and other sweets, offers a tour that puts visitors right on the factory floor. The visit lasts about an hour and includes a video. Everybody is given a hair net to wear and for safety reasons, children under five must be in a stroller. This is a working factory.

➻ Year-round: Mon—Fri, except major holidays. Walk-in tours (without reservations) are conducted at 2 pm. Reserved tours can be scheduled as early as 8:45 am. Plan several days in advance especially around school holidays.

➻ Free.

➻ Take I-90/94 north. Continue north on I-94 (it becomes U.S. 41) to the Buckley Rd. Exit. Go east on Buckley to Lewis Ave. and turn north. At 24th St. (the first stop sign) turn east and continue on (24th becomes Morrow Ave.) to the factory; it's just after the railroad tracks.

Eli's Cheesecake Factory

6701 W. Forest Preserve Dr., Chicago
(773) 736-3417
www.elicheesecake.com

Eli's, "The Place For Steak," is a famous restaurant in the Loop that gave birth to an even more famous dessert—Eli's Cheesecake. At Eli's Cheesecake World visitors get to see how these decadent pleasures are developed, hand-made and decorated. You'll also enjoy a sample. Eli's offers different tour packages, from the basic Sneak Peak Tour to the Ultimate Eli's Experience, which includes lunch and a personally decorated cake.

➤ Year-round: Mon—Fri (by appointment), 10 am—3 pm. A walk-in tour is conducted at noon.

➤ Cost varies with the tour. Sneak Peak Tour: Adults $3, children (under 12) $2. Ultimate Eli's Experience: $22.50 per person.

➤ Take I-90/94 west to the Irving Park Rd. Exit. Travel west on Irving Park to Narragansett Ave. Turn north on Narragansett to Montrose Ave. Turn west on Montrose to Forest Preserve Dr. and travel south.

Chicago Board of Trade
141 W. Jackson Blvd., Chicago
(312) 435-3590
www.cbot.com

Chicago is an important financial center. Why not take your family to see the wheeling and dealing that goes at the Chicago Board of Trade? From the Visitor's Center, you can observe the frenzied action on the trading floor below, then take-in an educational presentation about the markets. A film entitled *A Window on Futures* helps kids to understand what's actually going on, and a small museum offers a historical glimpse of commodity trading.

➤ Year-round: Mon—Fri, 8 am—2 pm. Educational presentations are scheduled every 30 minutes beginning at 9:15 am with the final one given at 12:30 pm.

➤ Free.

➤ Take Van Buren St. or Adams St. heading west. The Board of Trade is on Jackson Blvd., which is one way heading east. Park in one the pay parking garages after you cross Clark St. The Quincy, LaSalle and Jackson El stops are all near the Board of Trade.

CHAPTER 6

MUSIC, THEATER, DANCE AND CINEMA

Introduction

Culture is alive in Chicago and there are plenty of places where you and your children can see it first hand. If your kids are musically inclined, start by visiting the Chicago Symphony's ECHO Learning Center, where they'll have a blast discovering the basics of music via computers. If they liked that experience, they'll love taking music classes at the Old Town School of Folk Music. The Chicago Center for the Performing Arts Training Center offers classes in music and acting. Or sign them up for improv classes at the Second City Players Workshop.

Wondering about a venue where you can introduce your children to live theater? Look no further than Lifeline Theater or Emerald City Theater. Both companies specialize in staging engaging productions for kids. Ballet anyone? Nothing gets ballet lovers into the holiday spirit faster than a performance of *The Nutcracker*—especially if your child is one of the dancers!

Tricks of the Trade
CHICAGO CENTER FOR THE PERFORMING ARTS TRAINING CENTER

777 W. Green, Chicago
(312) 327-2040
www.theaterland.com

T he Chicago Center for the Performing Arts (an entertainment complex in the River North neighborhood) offers an ambitious schedule of music and theater courses at its Training Center.

For young thespians, there are currently 20 different classes with titles such as Musical Theater, Theater Games and On Camera Technique. Students, grouped by age, level of expertise and area of interest, are taught acting fundamentals and basic communication skills. They'll also learn how to broaden their emotional range. Even preschoolers get into the fun with Creative Play sessions. Classes meet two hours a week for eight weeks.

If your kids like music, consider enrolling them in EarlyBirds. It uses active participation to introduce children (newborns to five years) to the world of music over 12 weeks.

Looking for summer fun? The Training Center has plans for a summer camp to instruct kids as young as five in performance basics, musical theater, stagecraft and other theatrical elements. Students will put on a performance following the four-week camp.

SEASONS AND TIMES
➤ Class schedules vary. Visit the website for details.

COST
➤ Classes range from $135 to $250.

GETTING THERE
➤ By car, take Michigan Ave. north to Ontario St. Go west on Ontario to Orleans St. and turn north to Chicago Ave. Travel west on Chicago to Green St., then turn south. Free street parking in the area. The pay lot beside the building is free after 3:30 pm. About 15 minutes from Grant Park.
➤ By public transit, take the Blue line El towards O'Hare and get off at the Chicago Ave. station. Walk 2 blocks east to Green St. and then head south.

COMMENT
➤ Children serious about acting can audition for professional classes in the Up and Coming series that prepare youth for acting careers.

Make Your Own Music
ECHO LEARNING CENTER

**Symphony Orchestra Center
220 S. Michigan Ave., Chicago
(312) 294-3000
www.echo.cso.org**

Kids love making music. It comes naturally to them. At ECHO, the Chicago Symphony Orchestra's interactive music learning center, children create their own music and easily pick up basic composition.

ECHO's A-Musing Room features a series of high-tech lesson booths. Youngsters are given an "instrument box" to bring with them when they visit each booth. There are five in all; each with a different musical concept to learn—from Mapping and Recording to Sounds and Silence. Kids plug the box (it has a built-in computer) into the computers inside the booths and then manipulate colorful touch screens that operate the computers giving the lessons. Each lesson is eight minutes long and interactive. As they follow along, young composers create their own songs—with the help of the box. After the five booths have been visited, eager students plug their boxes into the Orchestra Wall to hear their compositions incorporated into a symphony performance. This is a fun, fast-paced way for kids to learn musical basics in less than an hour.

SEASONS AND TIMES
➤ Year-round: Tue–Sat, 10 am–5 pm; Sun, 11 am–5 pm. Call ahead to check on availability.

COST
➤ Adults $5.50, children $2.50.

GETTING THERE
➤ By car, take Michigan Ave. north to Adams St. and turn west. A pay garage is on the north side of Adams 1/2 block west of Michigan. Enter the Symphony Center through the Adams entrance. Less than 5 minutes from Grant Park.
➤ By public transit, take any El that circles the Loop to the Jackson stop. Walk north on Wabash St. to Adams and enter the Symphony Center.

NEARBY
➤ Art Institute, Grant Park, Spertus Institute.

COMMENT
➤ The A-Musing Room is intended for children 8 and up, though those as young as 6 will enjoy it. Everyone loves playing the percussion instruments in the entrance.

Green Eggs for Kids
EMERALD CITY
THEATER COMPANY

2936 N. Southport Ave., Chicago
(773) 529-2690
www.emeraldcitytheatre.com

Emerald City Theater Company is a great place to expose children to live theater. The company is dedicated to staging family-friendly shows directed and performed by professionals. The plays are often adaptations of familiar children's tales, usually with a funny twist or two and an educational message.

One long-running favorite is an off-beat, musical adaptation of Dr. Seuss' *Green Eggs & Ham*. Emerald City's show goes well beyond the standard re-telling of this story, and includes lots of improv and audience participation tossed into the mix. The play ends with a Seuss-like improvisational story created with the help of kids in the audience. Other recent shows have included *Noah's Ark, Frosty the Snowman* and *Cinderella*, each with a special Emerald City twist.

All of the plays are geared toward various age groups, from three-year-olds on up.

SEASONS AND TIMES
➤ Vary with the show. Visit the website for details.

COST
➤ Adults $10, children $8.

GETTING THERE
➤ Most performances are at the Apollo Theater, 2540 N. Lincoln Ave.
➤ By car, take Lake Shore Dr. N. to the Fullerton Ave. Exit. Travel west on Fullerton to Lincoln Ave. Turn north and drive 3 blocks to the theater. Street and lot parking (beside the theater). About 30 minutes from Grant Park.
➤ By public transit, take the Brown or Red line El to the Fullerton stop. Walk east 1 block on Fullerton to Lincoln Ave. then north 3 blocks to the theater.

COMMENTS
➤ If your kid loves theater, arrange a birthday party in conjunction with a performance by Emerald City.

Putting Your Best Foot Forward
JOFFREY BALLET CHICAGO

Suite 1300, 70 E. Lake St., Chicago
(312) 739-0120
www.joffrey.com

J offrey Ballet Chicago is an extraordinary professional ballet company that performs in Chicago and tours the country. One of their most popular performances is the holiday staple, *The Nutcracker*. This compelling story, with seasonal glitter and bits of magic, is a great way to introduce children to dance. The setting is of the Currier & Ives variety, with gorgeous period costumes and fantastic sets. Attending one of the company's 30-plus performances at the Auditorium Theater (30 E. Congress St.) will put your kids in the real holiday spirit.

Children can do more than watch the performances. They can dance in them. Each year Joffrey casts over 100 Chicago-area children as dancers in its performances of *The Nutcracker*. Visit the Joffrey website for audition information.

SEASONS AND TIMES
→ Performances of *The Nutcracker* run from late November to late December, with several shows each week. Call the number above or visit the website for details.

COST
➤ Tickets range from $8 to $55 per person.

GETTING THERE
➤ By car, the Auditorium Theater is located 1 block west of Michigan Ave. on Congress St., which runs into Grant Park. A pay parking garage is across the street from the theater.
➤ By public transit, CTA buses 10 and 146 stop in front of the theater.

COMMENT
➤ Read *The Nutcracker* and the *Mouse King* (the original tale by Ernst Theodor Amadeus Hoffman) before seeing the performance to increase your children's enjoyment.

The Sound of Music
KRAFT FAMILY
MATINEE SERIES

Chicago Symphony Orchestra
220 S. Michigan Ave., Chicago
(312) 294-3000
www.echo.cso.org

The Chicago Symphony Orchestra is one of Chicago's cultural crown jewels. Kids can witness the sparkle by attending a performance by the symphony.

The Kraft Family Matinee Series is designed to expose children to the beauty of classical music in a manner that's fun and welcoming. Each concert features familiar tunes for children—*Peter and the Wolf* was a recent performance; the music to *ET: The Extraterrestrial* was part of another—with dancers, actors and mimes joining the orchestra on stage. Even adults love the shows.

The Symphony, together with the Lyric Opera and the Joffrey Ballet, also takes part in a series of "sampler" concerts at the American Girl Theater (page 28).

SEASONS AND TIMES
➛ Certain Saturdays. Call for specific dates and times.

COST
➛ Tickets range from the low $20s to $40s, depending on section.

GETTING THERE
➛ By car, take Michigan Ave. north to Adams St and turn west. There is a pay garage on the north side of Adams 1/2 block west of Michigan. Less than 5 minutes from Grant Park.
➛ By public transit, take any El that circles the Loop to the Jackson stop. Walk north on Wabash St. to Adams then east to Michigan. Go south on Michigan to the entrance.

NEARBY
➛ Art Institute, Grant Park, Spertus Institute.

COMMENT
➛ The Kraft series is designed for families, but appropriate behavior is still expected of kids.

In the Spotlight
LIFELINE THEATRE

6912 N. Glenwood Ave., Chicago
(773) 761-4477
www.theatrechicago.com/lifeline

This cozy theater in the Rogers Park neighborhood puts on the KidSeries collection of popular children's plays. These well-loved presentations have earned the company "Best Children's Theater" designation from at least two Chicago news organizations.

The cheerful, professional cast knows how to get their young audiences interested in the performance, using lots of enthusiastic acting and raucous on-stage antics. Kids eat this stuff up. Truth be told, even adults enjoy the shows. Most are adaptations of children's books, such as *Ferdinand the Bull* and *The Emperor's Groovy New Clothes*.

Don't worry about occupying your kids if you arrive before show time. The lobby is a fun place to hang out, with a gigantic easy chair, colorful decorations and a small snack bar. A party room is available for kids desiring a theatrical birthday party.

SEASONS AND TIMES
➤ The KidSeries is performed in the spring and fall. Call for exact dates and times.

COST

➤ Adults and children, each performance $7.

GETTING THERE

➤ By car, take Lake Shore Dr. north (it becomes Sheridan Rd.) to Morse Ave. Turn west on Morse (go past Glenwood northbound). Immediately after the El tracks, turn onto Glenwood southbound and drive to the theater. For the free parking lot: turn onto northbound Glenwood before the El tracks. Take it to Estes Ave. and turn west. The lot is at the corner of Estes and Glenwood (southbound). From there, walk 3 blocks south to the theater. About 40 minutes from Grant Park.

➤ By public transit, take the Red line El north to the Morse Ave. stop. Exit the station on the west side of the tracks and walk 1 block south on Glenwood.

COMMENT

➤ The KidSeries plays are short and fast-paced so younger kids won't get bored.

Dance Your Heart Out at
LOU CONTE
DANCE STUDIO

Hubbard Street Dance Company, 1147 W. Jackson Blvd.,
Chicago
(312) 850-9766
www.hubbardstreetdance.com

Hubbard Street Dance Company is one of the most innovative modern dance companies in America. Aspiring dancers can tap into the wealth of talent at Hubbard Street by taking classes at the Lou Conte Dance Studio. The studio, which is named after the founder of Hubbard Street Dance Company, is staffed by active professional dancers who lead classes in jazz, tap, hip-hop, ballet and other styles. Seven levels are available, from courses for beginners to classes for professionals.

SEASONS AND TIMES
➤ Year-round. Course times vary; call for details.

COST
➤ Students can take one class for $12, or buy class "cards" that range in price from $105 (10 classes) to $360 (40 classes).

GETTING THERE
➤ By car, take I-290 W. to the Ashland Ave. Exit. Travel north on Ashland to Jackson Blvd. Turn east on Jackson to Racine Ave. The studio is at the corner of Jackson and Racine. Pay parking on site ($4). About 15 minutes from Grant Park.
➤ By public transit, take the Blue line El (towards Forest Park) to the Racine stop. Use the east exit from the station, and walk north on Racine to the studio.

COMMENT
➤ Proper footwear, such as jazz, tap or ballet shoes, is required depending on the class.

Pickin' and Grinnin'
OLD TOWN SCHOOL
OF FOLK MUSIC

4544 N. Lincoln Ave. and 909 W. Armitage Ave., Chicago
(773) 728-6000
www.oldtownschool.org

Chicago's Old Town School is renowned for helping keep Chicago's folk music, dance and theater scene vibrant since it opened in 1957. Part of the school's secret is in its ability to attract kids to the performing arts by offering them a complete range of courses in music, dance, art and theater.

If your kids like beating a rhythm on your kitchen pots, enroll them in the Little Drummers class. They'll explore percussion instruments and learn about rhythm and the importance of listening. If dance is your child's thing, try the Jitterbugs class, Yoga for Children, or Pre-ballet. Budding artists enjoy Squeeze & Pound, a beginner sculpting class for six- and seven-year-olds. Little actors are accommodated with a series of original musical productions developed and directed by Old Town School teachers. Each 12-week session ends with a performance for family and friends.

Old Town School also runs a summer camp program. These four or eight-week sessions introduce children ages 5 to 11 to music, dance, art and/or theater. Private lessons in many disciplines are available at the school.

SEASONS AND TIMES
➤ The school is open year-round. Visit the website for class and camp schedules.

COST
➤ Costs vary with the program. Full-day summer camp (4 weeks) is $750; the musicals (12 weeks) are $200; and the Squeeze & Pound sculpting class (8 weeks) costs $100.

GETTING THERE
Lincoln Ave. location
➤ By car, take I-90/94 N. to the Western Ave. Exit. Travel north on Western to Montrose Ave. and turn east. At Lincoln Ave. turn north to the school. Pay parking lot across the street. About 40 minutes from Grant Park.

➤ By public transit, take the Brown line El to the Western Ave. stop. Walk east under the tracks to Lincoln Ave., then south to the school.

Armitage Ave. location
➤ By car, take Lake Shore Dr. north to the Fullerton Ave. Exit. Travel west on Fullerton to Halsted St., turn south and drive to Armitage Ave. Turn west on Armitage to the school. Limited street parking (metered). About 25 minutes from Grant Park.

➤ By public transit, take the Brown line El north to the Armitage stop. Walk east to the school.

NEARBY
➤ Armitage location (boutiques and restaurants), Lincoln location (Lincoln Square, Welles Park).

COMMENT
➤ The Different Strummer music store, situated inside each Old Town School location, has affordable instrument rentals.

Kids Improv
PLAYERS WORKSHOP
OF THE SECOND CITY

2936 N. Southport Ave., Chicago
(773) 929-6288
www.playersworkshop.com

C hicago's Second City Theater is famous for its hilarious improvisational skits. Just as famous are alumni of its renowned Players Workshop—Bill Murray, Shelley Long and Bonnie Hunt to name a few.

Do your kids have stars in their eyes? They can literally get into the act by taking one of the improvisation classes offered by the Players Workshop. These four-week sessions are geared for youths ages 8 to 16 and take place at Lincoln Park Cultural Center (2045 N. Lincoln Park W.).

Professional actors lead the kids in exercises designed to emphasize creativity, improvisation and the ability to think quickly. Kids also learn how to communicate effectively. Students meet for 90 minutes each week for a month.

The Workshop also produces shows for young audiences, which it presents at various local theaters. Call the number above or visit the website for details.

SEASONS AND TIMES

➤ Classes are held on Saturdays; call for starting dates. 8 to 12 year olds meet from 10 am— 11:30 am; 13 to 16 year olds meet from 11:45 am— 1:15 pm.

COST

➤ $60 per child for a 4-week session.

GETTING THERE

➤ **Lincoln Park Cultural Center:**

By car, take Lake Shore Dr. north to the LaSalle/North Ave. Exit. Travel west on LaSalle Dr. to Clark St. Turn north and take that until it forks to the right onto Lincoln Park W.

NEARBY

➤ Lincoln Park, Lincoln Park Zoo, Peggy Notebaert Nature Museum.

COMMENT

➤ Classes run continuously and students may continue them for as long as they like.

Other Places to Visit

Chicago International Children's Festival

Facets Multimedia
1517 W. Fullerton Ave., Chicago
(773) 281-9075
www.cicff.org

Got a young movie buff in the family? Then you won't want to miss this ten-day extravaganza of children's cinema. It features close to 180 movies from around the world screened at two downtown venues. Better still, the festival offers kids a hands-on introduction to the business of film-making at its Take One! Workshop. Read more about the festival and workshops on (page 217) of this guide.

CHAPTER 7

ANIMALS, FARMS & ZOOS

Introduction

C hicago is urban to the core, but it does offer plenty of opportunity for animal lovers to observe wildlife. Start your adventure at either of Chicago's two world-class zoos: Brookfield or Lincoln Park. They are among the best anywhere, both in exhibit quality and conservation work. If marine life is more to your fancy, spend time among the coral reefs, dolphin shows and Amazon River banks at Shedd Aquarium. There are less elaborate displays to visit, too, from the tiny zoo at Indian Boundary Park on the Far North Side to the Hal Tyrell Trailside Museum in west suburban River Forest. If you want to really get your hands on wildlife, visit one of the many petting zoos in the distant suburbs, or wet a worm in one of the area's many fishing spots.

NOTE
Kids can see more animals at:
Peggy Notebaert Nature Museum (Chapter 2, page 45)

Animal Adventures
BROOKFIELD ZOO

3300 Golf Rd., Brookfield
(708) 485-0263
www.brookfieldzoo.org

Brookfield Zoo is world famous for its animal conservation research work and for the experience it offers visitors. Brookfield is home to thousands of animals living in enclosures sensitive to their natural needs while offering patrons maximum viewing enjoyment. You can find something new and interesting each time you visit.

Start your animal adventure with a romp through The Swamp. This indoor exhibit puts kids in the bayou complete with a swamp boat ride, views of alligators and other swamp life and loads of buttons and hands-on diversions for little fingers. Next door, Tropic World is a cavernous building with primate environments representing Asia, South America and Africa. A path high above the action wanders through the exhibits, allowing visitors to see scores of the furry animals living in a near-natural setting.

The Living Coast gives kids a close-up, sometimes wet look at marine life. Everyone is a bit startled when the tremendous waves crash into a plexi-glass panel above their heads in the tide pool exhibit. They are just as surprised to see sea birds flying about in the open!

Kids can feel the soft hair of young goats and other docile creatures in the petting zoo. The frequent Dolphin Shows are also a hit with all ages. Brookfield offers a complete line-up of educational opportunities for kids who want to immerse themselves in animal life. There is a series of fun holiday events for the whole family.

SEASONS AND TIMES
➤ Summer (June—Aug): Daily, 9:30 am—6 pm. Winter (Nov—Mar): Daily, 10 am—5 pm. Spring (Apr—May) and Fall (Sept—Oct): Mon—Fri, 10 am—5 pm; Sat—Sun, 10 am—6 pm.

COST
➤ Adults $7, seniors and children (3 to 11) $3.50, under 3 free. Free on Tuesdays and Thursdays, Oct—Mar.

GETTING THERE
➤ By car, take I-290 west to the 1st Ave. Exit. Travel south on 1st and follow the signs to the zoo's pay parking lot ($4). About 30 minutes from Grant Park.

NEARBY
➤ Wolf Road Prairie Nature Preserve, Oak Park Conservatory, Kiddieland.

COMMENT
➤ Brookfield Zoo has several excellent dining options, ranging from gourmet tapas to snack bars. Pack a lunch; there are plenty of picnic tables. Plan a 2- to 4-hour visit, depending on the stamina of your kids.

Wet a Worm
FISHING IN CHICAGO

East Branch of the Chicago River (between street numbers 300 and 400 N.), Chicago

Fishing in Chicago? You bet. In fact, the city hosted the Bass Grand Masters Championship Tournament in 2000.

There are two basic ways to fish in the Chicago area—charter a boat on Lake Michigan or fish from the shore. When the weather's fine, boat charters are a fun way to spend an afternoon. Don't be surprised if you reel in a large fish. Check out Captain Al's Charter Boat Fleet (312-565-0104), which launches from the harbor near McCormick Place in Chicago, or the Waukegan Charterboat Association (847-BIG-FISH) based in Waukegan, a suburb north of Chicago. Rods, reels, bait and safety equipment are supplied.

Fishing from the shore involves less time and expense. One popular spot that is easy to get to is the lagoon in Lincoln Park. You can catch bass and other sport fish by dropping a line anywhere along the shore. In the fall, adult fishermen snag mature salmon that drift up the lagoon in search of their spawning grounds, something your children might enjoy watching.

Other convenient fishing areas are around Montrose Harbor—the channel leading from the harbor and Lake Michigan itself. You can also try your luck from any of the piers along the lakeshore.

Just keep away from the beaches where hooks are a hazard to swimmers. Don't overlook the Chicago River. Bass fisherman plied the river waters regularly during the championships. A handy spot is a stretch of the Riverwalk between Michigan Avenue and Lake Shore Drive, on the south side of the river.

SEASONS AND TIMES
➤ Call the boat charters listed above for their hours of operation. The lakefront is always open to the public, but much of it freezes in winter.

COST
➤ Charter costs vary widely; call ahead for prices. A 24-hour fishing license costs $5.50. (Licenses are required for anyone over age 15 who is fishing and can be purchased at most sporting goods stores.)

COMMENT
➤ Most fish caught around the Chicago area are safe to eat, but family fishermen generally fish for fun, releasing what they catch. Discuss the benefits of practicing "catch and release"—the fish get to live and no one has to clean them—with your little fishermen before they catch that first fish.

Animal Survivors
HAL TYRELL TRAILSIDE MUSEUM

738 Thatcher Ave., River Forest
(708) 366-6530

Wounded wild animals have a safe haven at Hal Tyrell Trailside Museum. The building was constructed in 1874 as a finishing school for young ladies and became a museum in 1931. Since then, local residents have brought thousands of injured animals to Tyrell, where staffers work to rehabilitate them. If the animals can't be returned to the wild, they're cared for at the museum and put on exhibit to educate visitors.

Indoors, the beautiful old building is alive with the sounds of crows, blue jays and other birds cackling and calling from the rooms upstairs. Elsewhere, there are turtles, snakes, squirrels and other creatures too injured to live outdoors. Kids can touch deer antlers, examine ancient artifacts such as arrowheads found on the site and learn what owls eat by checking out their pellets. The museum's other displays focus on local wildlife and area history. The center's larger residents; owls, seagulls and a lively red fox, can be visited outdoors.

After you have seen the animals, go exploring. The museum's grounds are connected to Thatcher Woods, a forested area that spreads west from the museum to a small picnic area and north to the wooded trails on the other side of Chicago Avenue. The woods boast a large pond and a marshy area that demands exploration. If you're lucky, you may spot a deer, as this is one of the best places close to the city for seeing them.

SEASONS AND TIMES
➟ Year-round: Daily, 10 am—4 pm.

COST
➟ Free.

GETTING THERE
➟ By car, take I-290 west to the Harlem Ave. Exit. Travel north on Harlem to Chicago Ave. Turn west on Chicago until Thatcher Ave; the museum is located on the corner. There is a free parking lot off Chicago just past Thatcher. About 35 minutes from Grant Park.

NEARBY
➟ Frank Lloyd Wright Home and Studio, Oak Park Conservatory.

COMMENT
➟ Plan a 45-minute visit to the museum and another hour to explore the adjacent woods.

Tiny Zoo
INDIAN BOUNDARY PARK

2500 W. Lunt Ave., Chicago
(312) 742-7887
www.chicagoparkdistrict.com

T he Chicago Park District is generally not in the business of housing animals, but the small zoo inside Indian Boundary Park is the exception. Managed by Lincoln Park Zoo, this facility is tiny; housing a pair of mute swans, a white-tailed deer, a variety of goats and an alpaca. It's not a lot, but enough to provide residents and visitors to this Far North Side neighborhood with a little bit of animal life.

Indian Boundary Park, built on the site of an ancient Native settlement, is much more than a zoo. It features a gigantic wooden playground full of tunnels, staircases, balconies, towers, slides, ladders, balance beams and more. Volunteers built this amazing structure and it will keep your kids busy for hours. Beside the playground, a large sprinkling fountain is ideal for kids seeking relief on hot summer days. Head to the pretty pond occupying the eastern portion of the park and watch the ducks paddling about. There is an abundance of greenery along the shore. Don't pass up the opportunity to explore the field house. The beautiful architecture includes intricately carved chief heads and other interesting details.

Perhaps your children would like to celebrate their next birthday with a picnic in the park. Reservations are not required for small groups, although parties with more than 12 people should call the park office in advance.

SEASONS AND TIMES
➤ Park and zoo: Year-round, daily, dawn—dusk. The animals are outdoors for limited hours during winter.

COST
➤ Free.

GETTING THERE
➤ By car, take Lake Shore Dr. north until it ends. Follow the signs to Ridge Blvd. Take Ridge north until you go under railroad tracks. The street briefly ends at Ravenswood Pkwy. Follow Ravenswood north for about 2 blocks until Ridge resumes. Take Ridge to Lunt Ave. Turn west on Lunt and travel 5 blocks to the park. Free on-street parking surrounds the park. About 45 minutes from Grant Park.

➤ By public transit, take the Red line El north to the Morse stop, and transfer to CTA bus 96 (Lunt) going west to the park.

NEARBY
➤ Loyola University.

COMMENT
➤ The park was designed specifically without large open spaces. It is a quiet, tranquil place. Allow 20 minutes to see the zoo and an hour to enjoy the rest of the park.

Wild Adventures
LINCOLN PARK ZOO

Cannon Dr. at Fullerton Ave., Chicago
(312) 742-2000
www.lpzoo.com

A nimal lovers flock to Lincoln Park Zoo. It is a leading animal conservation study facility that displays species from around the world in authentic recreations of their natural habitats.

The adventure starts with elaborate outdoor exhibits, including the always-popular sea lion pool that has an underwater viewing room. Then there's the pond teeming with flamingoes, ducks and swans. At the elephant paddock kids sometimes have to dodge dust kicked up by the beasts' trunks.

More fun awaits indoors. The Small Mammal/ Reptile House puts kids in the midst of a steamy rain forest with monkeys swinging overhead and giant lizards below. Everyone enjoys watching the antics of the primates as they climb, tussle and hunt for snacks at the Ape House, made famous in the movie *Return to Me*. If seeing birds set your kids a flight, they'll never get enough of the inhabitants in the McCormick Bird House.

Kids love to touch animals. The zoo offers them opportunities to pet small ones, such as turtles and guinea pigs, at the Pritzker Children's Zoo and larger creatures, such as cows and goats, at the Farm-in-the-Zoo. For a change of pace, rent a paddle boat and cruise the lagoon at the south end of the zoo. Or let your kids romp in the elaborate playground outside the west gate.

SEASONS AND TIMES
➤ Spring (Apr 1—May 26): Daily, 8 am—6 pm. Summer (May 27—Sept 4): Mon—Fri, 8 am—6 pm; Sat—Sun, 8 am—7 pm. Fall (Sept 5—Oct 31): Daily, 8 am—6 pm. Winter (Nov 1—Mar 31): Daily, 8 am—5 pm.

COST
➤ Free.

GETTING THERE
➤ By car, take Lake Shore Dr. to the Fullerton Ave. Exit. Travel east for 2 blocks to Cannon Dr. The zoo's pay lot ($7) is at the corner. About 15 minutes from Grant Park.
➤ By bicycle or on foot, take the lakefront path to the Lake Shore overpass at North Avenue Beach. After you cross Lake Shore, head west to Cannon.

NEARBY
➤ Peggy Notebaert Nature Museum, Lincoln Park Conservatory, Chicago Historical Society.

COMMENT
➤ Don't hesitate to come in winter. There are fewer people and plenty of heated indoor habitats. Plan a 2-hour visit.

An Education in Animals
LITTLE RED SCHOOL HOUSE NATURE CENTER

**9800 S. Willow Springs Rd., Willow Springs
(708) 839-6897**

Apopular destination for school field trips, the Little Red School House Nature Center has lots for families too.

Built in 1886 and used as a classroom until 1948, this former one-room schoolhouse has a menagerie of live, indigenous animals used to teach visitors about local ecology. Kids can gander up close at snakes, turtles, raccoons and many other species. Knowledgeable staff will tell you about the exhibits. There are other displays to view, including one on Native arrowheads and another on plant seed dispersal.

Your indoor tour completed, head outside where the best part of the visit awaits. Bring binoculars and field guides as you hike on paths that wind through the center's 14,000 acres of woods and wetlands. There is plenty to see. Bugs, squirrels, animal tracks and all kinds of bird life are easy to spot. Curious kids will discover animal homes in hollow trees and spider webs dangling on fences.

The wetlands portion of the nature center is perhaps the biggest hit with children. Ducks and geese ply the waters and tall cattails crowd the shores. Come in the fall and see the amazing "boiling" waters—hordes of carp splashing about in the shallows.

If your kids are interested in learning about local ecology, attend one of the Little Red School House programs, which offer a more in-depth look at birds of prey, reptiles, small mammals and other wild residents.

SEASONS AND TIMES
➤ Trails: Mar–Oct, Mon–Fri, 8 am–5 pm; Sat–Sun, 8 am–5:30 pm. Nov–Feb, daily, 8 am–4:30 pm. Building: Mar–Oct, Mon–Thu, 9 am–4:30 pm; Sat–Sun, 8 am–5 pm. Nov–Feb, Sat–Thu, 9 am–4 pm. The entire center is closed on Thanksgiving, Christmas and New Year's.

COST
➤ Free.

GETTING THERE
➤ By car, take I-90/94 east to I-55. Go west on I-55 until the Willow Springs Rd. Exit. Travel south on Willow Springs until the school house. Free parking on site. About 1 hour from Grant Park.

COMMENT
➤ Plan a 2-hour visit.

Down on the Farm
PETTING ZOOS/ PICKING FARMS

Downtown Chicago is a concrete jungle, but an hour's drive west puts you in the middle of farm country. Opportunities abound to pick fruit and pumpkins at U-pick farms, with many including small petting zoos and other kid-friendly amusements. Also, at some of the farms you can cut your own Christmas tree.

Before packing the picnic lunch and loading up the kids, call ahead! Ask the following questions:

- Are you open today? Natural events such as storms and cold weather can curtail operations.
- What is available to pick today?
- How do I get there? You will require detailed directions as these farms are often off the main roads.

Visiting the farms are free. However, expect to pay close to or more than store prices for the fruit you pick or Christmas trees you cut, plus extra for snacks and entertainment. Wear grubby clothes, sturdy shoes and don't forget hats and sunblock in the summer. Leave your pets at home.

There are scores of farms within an hour of Chicago. The University of Illinois Extension Service website (www.urbanext.uiuc.edu) lists many of them. Here are a few to get you started.

Royal Oak Farm
15908 Hebron Rd., Harvard
(815) 648-2084

Royal Oak Farm is an apple picker's delight, with 10,000 apple trees sporting 25 varieties. There are also berries, peaches and a pumpkin patch. For the kids, this farm has an awesome play area with big climb-on vehicles including a pirate ship, train, tractor and much more. A petting area features all the popular barnyard animals.

➤ Open during the picking season. Mon—Sat, 9:30 am—5 pm. Varies with produce and weather.

Quig's Orchard
Rte. 83 (1/4 mile south of Midlothian Rd.), Mundelein
(847) 566-4520
www.quigs.com

Quig's Orchard features apples and pumpkins. You can pick apples during late summer and fall, but the real fun begins around mid-October when the Halloween festivities kick in. Features include the Haunted Barn and the Haunted Hayride, where live actors in spooky costumes try to scare your socks off. Younger kids love the Children's Pumpkin House, which offers entertainment geared for their enjoyment.

➤ Fall: Daily, 9 am—5 pm. Store and bakery, 7 am—5 pm. Restaurant, 7 am—2:30 pm.

Sycamore Pumpkin Patch
15436 Quigley Rd., Sycamore
(815) 895-3276

Sycamore specializes in pumpkins and features U-pick and pre-picked pumpkins. There is more here than just big orange squash. Your kids can romp through the Indian Village that has wigwams and artifacts. To get into the Halloween spirit, take your tykes through Haunted Forest and the corn maze, then let them pet the menagerie of farmyard animals. Wrap up your day with a hayride.

➤ Open most of Oct: Mon—Sat, 10 am—8 pm; Sun, 10 am—6 pm.

Among the Fishes
SHEDD AQUARIUM

1200 S. Lake Shore Dr., Chicago
(312) 939-2438
www.sheddnet.org

Before you visit Shedd Aquarium, toss out any images you have of little tanks of fish. This place is the real deal—massive aquariums containing complete ecosystems, walk-through exhibits, dolphin shows . . . everything having to do with marine life.

Begin your adventure at the Caribbean Reef exhibit, a gigantic cylindrical tank containing a coral reef. You'll see hundreds of colorful fish swimming laps around the reef, including a number of large sharks. Be sure you're there at feeding time when divers enter the tank to feed the fish and speak to audiences through a microphone. Kids especially enjoy manipulating a remote camera at the back of the tank.

The Shedd's newest exhibit, Amazon Rising, is a walk-through experiential display showing how animal and human communities living around the Amazon River deal with rising and falling water levels. It houses such Amazon denizens as piranhas and deadly bullet ants, and there are lots of hands-on, educational features that teach kids about the region and its wildlife.

Downstairs, the Oceanarium boasts a dolphin show, beluga whales, a tide pool and other fascinating exhibits. With so much to see, younger children might feel overwhelmed. Take them to Resource for the Curious, a small room where they can spend some quiet time with nature books, puppets and other playthings.

SEASONS AND TIMES
➤ Summer (Memorial Day–Labor Day): Daily, 9 am–6 pm. Winter: Daily, 9 am–5 pm. Closed Christmas and New Year's.

COST
➤ Adults $15, seniors and children (3 to 11) $11, under 3 free. Free on Mondays.

GETTING THERE
➤ By car, take Columbus Dr. south and follow the signs to Museum Campus and the aquarium. Three lots on Museum Campus charge $7 per car. About 5 minutes from Grant Park.

➤ By public transit, take the Red or Orange line El to the Roosevelt Rd./Museum Campus stop. From there, catch the Museum Campus trolley or CTA bus 12.
➤ By bicycle or on foot, follow the lakefront path south from the Loop.

NEARBY
➤ Field Museum, Adler Planetarium, Soldier Field, 12th St. Beach.

COMMENT
➤ There are coin-operated lockers for storing jackets. They are located down the stairs at the back of the main lobby on the right. Plan a 3-hour visit.

For the Love of Animals
WILLOWBROOK
WILDLIFE CENTER

One Park Blvd., Glen Ellyn
(630) 942-6200
www.dupageforest.com

Willowbrook Wildlife Center is a special gem. It is home to dozens of wounded animals that receive the attention of a caring staff and thousands of curious children during school field trips.

The animal hospital is located in the main building. Through large windows visitors can watch as caregivers feed and clean tiny abandoned babies and nurse larger wildlife back to health. Elsewhere in the hospital, you'll see creatures that have recovered from their injuries, including small birds, turtles and snakes. Foxes, eagles, owls and other larger patients are housed outside. Friendly, knowledgeable staff and descriptive panels tell visitors about the animals.

There are exhibits to study, too. The most poignant features a wall of a house that has numerous deterrents to keep wildlife from getting hurt, such as bird silhouette stickers on the windows and grates over the basement window wells. The center has a play area where younger visitors will find a sandbox with molds of animal feet that they can press into the sand to make prints. An animal puppet theater, a room with coloring paraphernalia and touch boxes containing animal pelts and bones round out the fun.

Behind the outdoor exhibits is a path leading to the Nature Trail. Follow this pleasant gravel-covered route and you'll go on a quick tour through common Illinois habitats—including marsh, prairie and savanna landscapes. Ungroomed trails lead more adventurous visitors deeper into these areas.

SEASONS AND TIMES
➝ Year-round: Daily, 9 am—5 pm. Closed Thanksgiving, Christmas Eve, Christmas Day and New Year's.

COST
➝ Free (donations accepted).

GETTING THERE
➝ By car, take I-290 west to Roosevelt Rd. Travel west on Roosevelt to Park Blvd. Take Park south until 22nd St. Free parking on site. About 1 hour from Grant Park.

NEARBY
➝ Morton Arboretum.

COMMENT
➝ Plan a 1-hour visit.

CHAPTER 8

GREEN SPACES

Introduction

C hicago's official motto is Urbs in Horto, which means city in a garden. Experience this motto first hand by visiting the beautiful green spaces in and around the city. Lincoln Park, with its majestic oak trees, groomed paths and broad open spaces, is a great place to start. Here you can watch ducks in the ponds, walk along the lakefront or let your kids romp in one of the many well-maintained play lots. Make your way over to the beaches, where your kids can build sandcastles or swim while you take in the awesome views. At North Park Village Nature Center, north of downtown, you can walk through a forest in the heart of the city.

A little farther away, children can see all kinds of flora and fauna while exploring Morton Arboretum's miles of trails, or spend an afternoon visiting the elaborate formal gardens of the Chicago Botanic Garden. For a taste of what the area was like before it was settled, check out the Wolf Road Prairie Nature Preserve. Don't worry if the weather's cold—three area conservatories offer amazing displays of plant life under glass. You'll soon think you are in Hawaii rather than Chicago!

NOTE

The following green spaces, which are covered elsewhere in this guide, are also ideal for a family outing:
Chicago River Walk (Chapter 1, page 19)
Grant Park/Lakefront (Chapter 1, page 23)
Hal Tyrell Trailside Museum (Chapter 7, page 135)
Indian Boundary Park (Chapter 7, page 137)
Little Red School House Nature Center (Chapter 7, page 141)
Willowbrook Wildlife Center (Chapter 7, page 147)

Sunny, Sandy and sometimes Windy
CHICAGO BEACHES

Various locations along Lake Michigan, Chicago
(312) 747-2200 (General Park District)
www.chicagoparkdistrict.com

C hicago's five-and-a-half miles of sandy beaches are truly among the city's hidden gems. With clean sand, fresh Lake Michigan water and mild breezes, a summer day on a Chicago beach rivals any island adventure. Depending where you are in the city, nearly every neighborhood along the lakefront has a sandy swimming beach that's supervised. Most feature changing rooms.

The most popular beaches for people downtown are Ohio Street Beach, Oak Street Beach and North Avenue Beach. Steps away from Navy Pier (page 30), Ohio Street Beach features a wide expanse of sand that's perfect for building castles. The water is shallow and there are expansive views of skyscrapers looming to the west. Oak Street Beach, about a half-mile north along the lakefront path, is famous for its beautiful people who live in nearby Gold Coast homes. North Avenue Beach (actually five beaches connected) reaches nearly to Fullerton Avenue. A newly renovated beach house shaped like a ship dominates the southern end and beach volleyball players occupy much of the sand in front of it. Yet there is always room for one more beach blanket.

When you have had enough swimming for one day, take your crew beachcombing—lots of interesting

shells and rocks get washed up on shore—or stroll
or bike along the lakefront paths (rentals at Navy
Pier). For a slower approach, buy a fruity ice bar
from one of the push cart vendors, sit back and
survey the action.

SEASONS AND TIMES
➤ You can walk on the beaches anytime, though they are officially
closed during winter.

COST
➤ Free.

GETTING THERE
Ohio Street Beach:
➤ By car, take Lake Shore Dr. north to the Illinois Ave. Exit. Follow
the signs to Navy Pier. Pay for parking on the pier and then walk
back towards the Loop on the footpath on the north side of the
pier. About 5 minutes from Grant Park.
➤ By public transit, take CTA bus 29 (State St.) or 65 (Grand Ave.)
to the pier's front entrance. In the summer, a free trolley travels
between Navy Pier and State. Catch it beside the "Navy Pier Trolley
Stop" signs.
Oak Street Beach:
➤ Use the directions to get to Ohio Street Beach, then walk north
along the lakefront path.
North Avenue Beach:
➤ By car, take Lake Shore north to the North Ave. Exit. There is a
meter parking lot at the beach or travel west to the underground
pay garage at the corner of North and Clark St. About 10 minutes
from Grant Park.
➤ By public transit, take CTA bus 151 (Sheridan) on State to North.
Walk east under the Lake Shore overpass until you reach the beach.

NEARBY
➤ Navy Pier, Lincoln Park Zoo, Peggy Notebaert Nature Museum.

COMMENT
➤ Spring and fall are wonderful times for beach excursions. There
are fewer people and the natural wonder of the lakefront is
magnified. Consider having a picnic party at the beach for your
child's next birthday.

Finery and Greenery
CHICAGO BOTANIC GARDEN

1000 Lake Cook Rd., Glencoe
(847) 835-5440
www.chicago-botanic.org

The Chicago Botanic Garden is a plant-lover's
paradise. Its 385 acres feature 23 meticulously
maintained gardens, information panels,
miles of walking trails and plenty of groomed open
spaces where you can lie back and relax.

Among the Garden's highlights is a large pond
stocked with fish, ducks and several islands. The Main
Island, reached by crossing a footbridge, houses most
of the gardens, including the kid-popular Aquatic
Garden. It boasts a boardwalk that runs over the
water, offering young visitors a view of the plants.

At the Circle Garden, patrons enjoy the seasonal
colors of annuals planted around a beautiful fountain. In the Sensory Garden, kids can experience
the smells, sounds, colors and textures of the plant
world. Exploring the six garden "rooms" in the
English Walled Garden is another fun stop for
children. Those with more of a wild streak might
enjoy the McDonald Woods & Nature Trail, located
off the Main Island near the parking lots, where

they can tromp about and see ungroomed nature up close. Wear bug repellent if you go in late spring and summer.

First-time visitors enjoy taking the Garden's tram ride that tours the facility with a live narrator. The School of the Botanic Garden offers a variety of classes for every age, on all things botanical.

SEASONS AND TIMES
➳ Year-round: Daily, 8 am—sunset. Closed Christmas.

COST
➳ Free.

GETTING THERE
➳ By car, take I-94 west/north to U.S. Rte. 41. Take Rte. 41 north to the Lake Cook Rd. Exit. Travel east for about 1/2 mile to the Garden.
➳ Pay parking on site ($7). About 1 hour from Grant Park.

NEARBY
➳ Ravinia Park.

COMMENT
➳ The Garden's very popular seasonal exhibits are well worth seeing. Plan a 2-hour visit.

Cultivating a Love for Plants
GARFIELD PARK CONSERVATORY

**300 N. Central Park Ave., Chicago
(312) 746-5100
www.garfield-conservatory.org**

Conservatories are fun green spaces to visit because of their lushness and variety of interesting plant life, but Garfield Park Conservatory offers something extra: a room dedicated to children.

The Elizabeth Morse Genius Children's Garden is partially educational and entirely fun for kids. A giant recreated root leads them along a path that stops at interesting displays. The first, an enormous seed with windows, enables youngsters to see what a developing seedling looks like. Next, they'll visit an oversized leaf lying on its back with a "sun" overhead. Turn a crank and the sun slowly spins and dribbles out yellow balls representing sunlight, which are "absorbed" by holes in the leaf. The path continues up a short flight of stairs, where the root is connected to a gigantic stem and flower. Turn another crank and a huge bee gently glides into the blossom! This exhibit is a fun and intelligent way to explain basic botany to children.

The rest of the conservatory, Chicago's largest, should not be overlooked. Kids will especially enjoy the Fern Room featuring rock tunnels crowded with thousands of leafy ferns and a pool that is home to a family of turtles and huge goldfish. In this steamy, lush environment it doesn't take much imagination to believe that a dinosaur is surely around the next corner.

SEASONS AND TIMES
➤ Year-round: Daily, 9 am—5 pm.

COST
➤ Free.

GETTING THERE
➤ By car, take I-290 west to the Independence Ave. Exit. Drive north on Independence until Washington Blvd. Turn east on Washington and travel to Central Park Ave. Turn north on Central Park and continue until the conservatory. Free parking on site. About 30 minutes from Grant Park.

COMMENT
➤ This place entertains adults as much as kids. Plan a 90-minute visit.

Chicago's Jewel
LINCOLN PARK

**From North Ave. to Ardmore St.
at the lakefront, Chicago
(312) 747-2200 (General Park District)
www.chicagoparkdistrict.com**

Named after Abraham Lincoln, Lincoln Park stretches along the lakefront through the heart of Chicago's North Side and is considered the premier green space in the city. The area was mostly marshland in Chicago's early days and later parts of it housed a cemetery. But rolling hills, giant trees, miles of paths, flower gardens and several small bodies of water make this park a beautiful natural patch in the city, where visitors can bike, hike, swim or cross-country ski. Lincoln Park Zoo (page 139) and the Peggy Notebaert Nature Museum (page 45) are found here and there is miniature golf, a driving range and other amusements too.

Lincoln Park's four playgrounds attract little kids. A large, modern play lot immediately outside the southwest gate of Lincoln Park Zoo features a solid jungle gym, a sand pit, swings and statues of an elephant and an orangutan that children can climb. Beside the miniature golf course off Diversey Avenue is another well-equipped playground, shaded with enormous oak trees and boasting wooden balance beams. Just to the north, a third play lot has older, more charming equipment, such as a fast slide with a parallel staircase and a huge sandbox. If it's a hot day, make sure your kids have their swimsuits so they can run through the water sprinklers. The sandy digging area, spinning "gerbil" wheel and "telephone tubes" make the fourth play lot at the north end of North Pond well worth the walk.

SEASONS AND TIMES
➤ Year-round: Daily, dawn—dusk.

COST
➤ Free.

GETTING THERE

➤ By car, take Lake Shore Dr. north to the LaSalle/North Ave. Exit. Travel west on LaSalle to the garage on the corner of Clark St. and LaSalle. About 15 minutes from Grant Park.

➤ By public transit, take any CTA bus running along Lake Shore Dr. The Red line El travels parallel to the park, but the distances of the stations to the park range from 1/2 to 1 mile.

NEARBY

➤ Lincoln Park Zoo, Peggy Notebaert Nature Museum, Chicago Historical Society, beaches.

COMMENT

➤ If you're into team sports, you can find games of softball, rugby and soccer being played in Lincoln Park. Plan a 4-hour visit.

Green Under Glass
LINCOLN PARK CONSERVATORY

2400 N. Stockton Ave., Chicago
(312) 742-7736

The Lincoln Park Conservatory is the perfect green escape from a winter day and a quiet diversion from the more raucous activities of Lincoln Park (page 156). Built in 1892, the conservatory's soaring glass domes provided year-around green space for Victorian Chicagoans.

The entrance to the main room, with its pleasant, small pond backed by beautiful flowers in bloom, sets the mood for the rest of the visit. Follow the path to the right and you enter a jungle scene with tropical plants towering high above and exotic flowers of every shape and color at eye level. Panels throughout the exhibits identify most of the plants. Exit the main room at the back to enter the fern room, a place that is alive with trickling water and festooned with dangling plants apparently growing from the ceiling. Kids will want to linger at the small waterfalls and streams that humidify the room. Behind the fern room is another room with a small pond supporting water plants and goldfish. Beside this is the exhibition room, where the conservatory houses its temporary displays. Everyone will be enchanted as the small train winds its way through myriad plants and streams, past tiny buildings made of thatch, sticks and other natural products.

The conservatory hosts seasonal exhibitions when you can take in colorful arrangements of Christmas poinsettias and spring flowers.

SEASONS AND TIMES
➤ Year-round: Sat—Thu, 9 am—5 pm; Fri, 9 am—9 pm.

COST
➤ Free.

GETTING THERE
➤ By car, take Lake Shore Dr. to the Fullerton Ave. Exit. Drive west on Fullerton to Stockton Ave. The conservatory is on the corner of Fullerton and Stockton. You can park along the street or in the Lincoln Park Zoo lot, just east of the conservatory at Cannon Dr. About 20 minutes from Grant Park.

NEARBY
➤ Lincoln Park Zoo, Peggy Notebaert Nature Museum.

COMMENT
➤ The formal gardens and fountain in front of the conservatory are a delightful place to take a breather. Plan a 1-hour visit.

Unending Trails
MORTON ARBORETUM

4100 Illinois Rte. 43, Lisle
(630) 968-0074
www.mortonarb.org

This grand monument to botany is a fantastic place for people who like communing with nature. Covering 1,700 acres (including many that are ungroomed and cater to a child's sense of adventure), Morton Arboretum has 12 miles of marked paths to hike. The arboretum is divided in half by Route 53; the eastern section houses the Visitor Center, with a gift shop, restaurant, picnic area and trail maps and plant guides to take with you on your walk. If you follow the trails leading from the Visitor Center, you'll wander through a variety of forests, past a large pond and into some open areas where the kids can frolic.

To get to the west side of the arboretum, take the single foot path that snakes from the east side of the parking lot under Route 53. A popular walk is the Joy Path, which begins at the Thornhill Education Center and meanders past a lush perennial garden and open woodland area, petering out in a crabapple orchard. Also on the west side is what is arguably the arboretum's most popular section: Schulenberg Prairie. This expertly recreated bit of Illinois prairie reclaimed from farmland features tall, waving grasses, colorful wildflowers and other native plants. It's a great place to spot butterflies and birds.

For an orientation to the grounds, ride the Acorn Express, an open-air tram that gives one-hour tours with live narration (April through October, Wednesdays and weekends). Morton Arboretum offers more than an afternoon diversion. This world-renowned research center also has educational programs—from the Nature Explorer day camps for kids to professional landscaping training. Information on the programs is available at the Visitor Center.

SEASONS AND TIMES
➤ Early Apr–late Oct: Daily, 7 am–7 pm. Late Oct–early Apr: Daily, 7 am–5 pm.

COST
➤ $7 per car ($3 per car on Wed).

GETTING THERE
➤ By car, take I-290 west to I-88 and continue west until Rte. 83. Take the north Exit for 83. The Arboretum is immediately north of it. Free parking on site. About 1 hour from Grant Park.

NEARBY
➤ Willowbrook Wildlife Center, Cantigny Park.

COMMENT
➤ The gift shop has some great gifts for science-minded children. Bring insect repellent if you visit during bug season and hats and sunscreen in the summer. Plan a 3-hour visit.

Oasis in the City
NORTH PARK VILLAGE NATURE CENTER

5801 N. Pulaski Rd., Chicago
(312) 744-5472

North Park Village Nature Center is a natural oasis tucked away in the bustle of Chicago's Far North Side. Begin your visit at the administration building, which has hands-on displays about wildlife and nature. Kids can touch native animal antlers, bones and pelts; watch bees making honey in a real hive; and examine nature projects created by other children taking classes at the center. Down the hall, an activity room is chock-full with nature books, puzzles and coloring opportunities for younger kids.

The real action starts when you head outdoors and explore the paths on the center's grounds, which wind through wetlands, savanna, prairie and woodland habitats. In the wetland area, kids can spy crayfish and frogs from the elevated wooden sidewalk. Other animals, including deer and raccoons, come here too, and you'll see their footprints in the mud.

Keep your eyes peeled for small toads bouncing through wood chips and squirrels collecting nuts in the savanna and woodland portions of the trail. Tall grasses and flowers dominate the prairie habitat, which is the perfect spot for kids who like to chase butterflies and other bugs.

Don't overlook the gardens in front of the building. They feature a variety of plant life, from Native American medicinal herbs to vegetables you'd cultivate in your own garden. Call the center about its nature classes for children or inquire while you're there.

SEASONS AND TIMES
➤ Year-round: Daily, 10 am—4 pm. Closed Easter, Thanksgiving, Christmas and New Year's.

COST
➤ Free. Some programs have nominal fees.

GETTING THERE
➤ By car, take I-90/94 west to the Pulaski Rd. Exit. Travel north on Pulaski for about 2 1/2 miles. The Nature Center is within North Park Village, which is on the east side of Pulaski. Free parking on site. About 45 minutes from Grant Park.

COMMENT
➤ Bring insect repellent if it's bug season and sunscreen and hats in the summer. Plan on spending at least 30 minutes at the displays and an hour on the trails.

Suburban Horticulture
OAK PARK CONSERVATORY

617 Garfield St., Oak Park
(708) 386-4700

O ak Park, a historic suburb on the western border of Chicago, features a small conservatory that's part of the area's history. The conservatory got its start in 1914 when local residents, (Ernest Hemingway, Frank Lloyd Wright, Edgar Rice Burroughs, Ray Kroc and other famous folk have lived here over the years) brought back plants from their vacations overseas and donated them to the town.

Children especially enjoy visiting the main room, which resembles a soaring rain forest. Banana trees with real bananas hanging in bunches compete for space with massive palms and other exotic plants. A stone bridge crosses a pretty little pond in the middle of the room and kids can't miss spotting giant goldfish and the occasional turtle swimming about. A tiny waterfall trickles along the east wall of this room, spilling into a stream that visitors can cross by stepping on rocks.

The cactus room, a dry, warm space filled with an amazing array of spiked specimens, is another hit for the young set. A small corridor near the southeast corner of this room features a carnivorous plant display. You're bound to notice the conservatory's extensive exotic bird collection found throughout the building. These award-winners regularly greet visitors with "Hello!"

Meetings and seminars on plants are regularly held at the conservatory. Got a plant problem? Plant clinics are on Mondays from 2 to 4 pm.

SEASONS AND TIMES
➤ Year-round: Mon, 2 pm—4 pm; Tue, 10 am—4 pm; Wed—Sun, 10 am—6 pm.

COST
➤ Free (suggested donation of $1 per person).

GETTING THERE
➤ By car, take I-290 west to the Austin Ave. Exit. Turn south off the Exit, then west onto Garfield St. immediately past the overpass. Travel on Garfield to East Ave. The conservatory is on the southwest corner. Free street parking. About 20 minutes from Grant Park.
➤ By public transit, take the Blue line El toward Forest Park. Get off at the Oak Park Ave. stop, and walk east along the platform to the East Ave. Exit. You'll see the conservatory on your right when you leave the platform.

NEARBY
➤ Frank Lloyd Wright Home and Studio.

COMMENT
➤ Plan a 1-hour visit.

On Your Soapbox!
WASHINGTON
SQUARE PARK

**Bounded by Clark St., Delaware St., Dearborn Pkwy.
and Walton St., Chicago
(312) 747-2200 (General Park District)
www.chicagoparkdistrict.com**

I f you're downtown and seeking a little green
space, Washington Square Park—Chicago's
oldest park—is a good option. This small park,
which occupies one city block, was once called
Bughouse Square and hosted zealots on soap boxes
bent on converting passersby to their point of view.
Later it degenerated into squalor.

That's all changed. The city has renovated the
park in a big way by installing a large, classical
fountain in the center and encircling it with benches
where office workers eat lunch while enjoying the
view of the fountain and nearby Newberry Library.
People watching and dog walking are other popular
pastimes for park visitors.

The park beyond the fountain has rich, green
grass and large, shady trees that are ideal for a game
of tag or hide-and-seek, either before or after you
visit the Feet First Exhibit at the Scholl College of
Podiatric Medicine (page 47).

SEASONS AND TIMES
→ Year-round: Daily, dusk—dawn.

COST
➤ Free.

GETTING THERE
➤ By car, take State St. north to Delaware St. Look for metered street parking on Delaware and walk west to the park. About 15 minutes from Grant Park.
➤ By public transit, take the Red line El to the Chicago stop. Walk north on State to Delaware, then west to the park. Or catch CTA bus 22 on Dearborn Pkwy. in the Loop and take it north to the corner of Dearborn and Delaware.

NEARBY
➤ Feet First Exhibit at the Scholl College of Podiatric Medicine, Newberry Library, fast-food restaurants.

COMMENT
➤ This is a good place to chill out after a busy day doing the tourist thing in River North. Directly to the north of the park is Newberry Library, a renowned repository of important literature. Plan a 30-minute visit.

Go Wild Near the City
WOLF ROAD PRAIRIE
NATURE PRESERVE

Corner of Wolf Rd. and Westchester St., Westchester
(708) 771-1330

Visitors to the Wolf Road Prairie Nature Preserve can thank the Great Depression for the beauty of these secluded 44 acres just west of Chicago. In the 1920s, a developer bought the land to build homes. He even constructed a grid work of sidewalks throughout the lot, but when the stock market crashed, he was forced to abandon the project.

Fortunately, those sidewalks did not go to waste. Visitors to this prairie habitat now use them to navigate through the chest-high native grasses, which are reminiscent of the tall grass prairies that once covered most of Illinois. Kids who are into nature will enjoy the feeling of the vegetation brushing against them. The plant life is incredible to see—look for giant leaves that resemble sandpaper, gorgeous flowers of all hues and grasses that tower overhead. Everywhere, you'll observe butterflies, bees and other bugs servicing the blossoms. Bring your cameras, camcorders and binoculars and pack your field guides to identify the plants and animals you see.

The area also contains a marsh that's wet and swampy, and a savanna—a transition area between the deep woods and prairie harboring short, well-spaced trees and shrubs. There is no good place to picnic at the preserve; it's 100 percent wild. But just south on Wolf Road is the entrance to Bemis Woods where there are plenty of picnic tables. Bike riders and serious hikers can access the Salt Creek Trail from Bemis Woods.

SEASONS AND TIMES
➤ Year-round: Daily, dawn—dusk.

COST
➤ Free.

GETTING THERE
➤ By car, take I-290 west from Chicago and exit at 12/45 (LaGrange Rd.). Travel south on LaGrange to 31st St., then turn west and continue until you cross Wolf Rd. There is a tiny free parking lot on the north side of 31st St., about 50 yards west of Wolf. About 45 minutes from Grant Park.

NEARBY

➤ Bemis Woods, Brookfield Zoo.

COMMENT

➤ If it is a hot, sunny day remember to bring hats, sunscreen and plenty of liquids. At the north end of the prairie is an old house being restored as a nature center. Get there by traveling north on Wolf Rd. and then turn west on Constitution Dr. Plan a 1-hour visit.

CHAPTER 9

HISTORICAL SITES

Introduction

C hicago boasts a proud history, growing from a prairie outpost to major metropolis in little more than a century. There's no better way for children to learn about the history of the area than to visit the heritage and historical sites listed in this chapter. Begin with a walking tour through the early neighborhood of wealth in the Prairie Historic District. Two of the mansions are open for visits. Over the years, millions of immigrants made Chicago home. Learn about their legacy at the Jane Addams Hull House Museum and the Maxwell Street Market. To witness rural turn-of-the-century life, drive to Naper Settlement. The Chicago Water Tower, the Tribune Tower, Ernest Hemingway Museum, and Frank Lloyd Wright Home and Studio have their own stories to tell that not only engage your children, but have them asking for more.

NOTE
More history awaits children at these sites described elsewhere in this guide:
The Field Museum (Chapter 1, page 21)
First Division Museum at Cantigny (Chapter 2, page 35)
Chicago Historical Society (Chapter 2, page 37)
Lake County Discovery Museum (Chapter 5, page 100)

The Survivor!
CHICAGO WATER TOWER

806 N. Michigan Ave., Chicago
(312) 744-2400

The Chicago Water Tower was built in 1869 and is one of Chicago's most recognizable landmarks. Among its claims to fame—it was the only building in the area to withstand the Chicago Fire of 1871. In the ensuing years, the tower became an important reference point for Chicagoans.

No doubt the tower's construction (limestone blocks quarried in Illinois) was partly responsible for its survival. Designed by architect William Bovington to resemble a medieval castle, it stands 154 feet tall. As the city's first real municipal water tower, it served as a standpipe for Lake Michigan water pumped through a two-mile tunnel reaching far into the lake. In 1971, the tower and the pumping station across from it were designated Chicago historic landmarks.

The tower no longer stores drinking water. Now it houses the City Gallery which has ongoing exhibitions of works by Chicago photographers. More intriguing for kids is the quick trip across the street to the Pumping Station. They can see the gigantic pipes and machinery that still pump water to the downtown area.

SEASONS AND TIMES
➤ Year-round: Mon—Fri, 9:3o am—6 pm; Sat, 1o am—6 pm; Sun, noon—5 pm.

COST
➤ Free.

GETTING THERE
➤ By car, take Michigan Ave. north to the Water Tower. Pay parking in lots in the area. About 5 minutes from Grant Park.
➤ By public transit, ride any CTA bus that travels Michigan Ave.

NEARBY
➤ Magnificent Mile, Hancock Observatory, DisneyQuest, ESPN Zone™, American Girl Place.

COMMENT
➤ Plan a 1-hour visit. The Pumping Station features a Visitor Center, café and gift shop with curios such as Chicago street signs, parking meters and other used municipal equipment.

Hemingmania
ERNEST HEMINGWAY MUSEUM AND BIRTHPLACE

200 N. Oak Park Ave., Oak Park
(708) 848-2222
www.hemingway.org

Ernest Hemingway is one of Chicago's favorite and most famous sons. This much-celebrated novelist and short-story writer (he won the Pulitzer and Nobel prizes for Literature) spent his first 18 years in west suburban Oak Park. Hemingway's birthplace and museum offer visitors of all ages a fascinating look at this extraordinary man.

The museum is inside ornate Oak Park Arts Center and has personal possessions, artifacts and photographs that recount Hemingway's life. Did you know he loved to hunt and fish? Younger kids enjoy ogling his stuffed animal trophies and touching his canoe. They can also sit in an old-time school desk like the one he used as a student. Older visitors appreciate the museum's literary exhibits, such as Hemingway's childhood diary, the famous letter nurse Agnes von Kurowsky wrote to him terminating their relationship, and a display of first-edition book jackets. A video on Hemingway's high school years is interesting, as are scenes from movies adapted from his books.

Hemingway's birthplace is a beautiful Victorian home two blocks north of the museum (339 N. Oak Park Ave.). It's a hands-on place, giving kids a good feel for upper-middle-class life a century ago. They will be amazed to see how small the kitchen is—without a refrigerator. The other rooms reveal family photographs, furnishings and belongings.

SEASONS AND TIMES
→Year-round: Thu—Fri, 1 pm—5 pm; Sat, 10 am—5 pm; Sun, 1 pm—5 pm.

COST
→ Adults $6, children (6 to 17) $4.50, under 6 free (includes admission to the museum and the birth home).

GETTING THERE

➤ By car, take I-290 W. to the Harlem Ave. Exit. Take Harlem north to Lake St. Turn east on Lake to Oak Park Ave. and drive north to the museum. Some street parking and pay garages are nearby. About 20 minutes from Grant Park.

➤ By public transit, take the Green line El west to the Oak Park Ave. station. Walk north on Oak Park to the museum.

NEARBY

➤ Frank Lloyd Wright Home and Studio, Oak Park Conservatory.

COMMENT

➤ Plan a 2-hour visit. Afterwards, take the kids to romp at beautiful, spacious Scoville Park across from the museum. It features a playground and a World War I memorial with Hemingway's named inscribed on it.

Where Modern Architecture Began
FRANK LLOYD WRIGHT HOME AND STUDIO

951 Chicago Ave., Oak Park
(708) 848-1976
www.wrightplus.org

Renowned architect Frank Lloyd Wright turned building design on its head a century ago when he abandoned Victorian boxiness for the clean lines of the Prairie School of Design. Wright's Home and Studio in Oak Park offers visitors young and old a taste of the old master's work and life.

Wright lived with his family and worked in the Home and Studio from 1889 to 1909—the years in which he developed the Prairie style of architecture. His home was his laboratory where he experimented with light, form, materials, space and furnishings. You can see results of his trials in the mix of design elements found throughout the house.

If young kids are in your group, schedule your visit around a Junior Architecture Tour. These tours are guided by trained sixth- to tenth-graders and are specially designed for 6- to 14-year olds. For them, the most enjoyable part is seeing how the Wright children lived, including their bedrooms and an elaborate play room with a vaulted ceiling and intricate woodwork. Young visitors, and grown-ups too, get a kick seeing a real tree (not the original) growing in the middle of the house.

SEASONS AND TIMES
➤ Junior Architecture Tours: Fourth Saturday of each month, 10 am. Regular tours: Mon—Fri, 11 am, 1 pm and 3 pm; Sat—Sun, every 15 minutes between 11 am—3:30 pm.

COST
➤ Junior Architecture Tour: Adults and children $3. Regular tour: Adults $9, children (7 to 18) $7, under 7 free.

GETTING THERE
➤ By car, take I-290 W. to the Harlem Ave. Exit. Travel north on Harlem to Chicago Ave. Turn east on Chicago and drive to the studio. Free street parking available. About 20 minutes from Grant Park.
➤ By public transit, take the Green line El west to the Oak Park Ave. station. Walk north on Oak Park 5 blocks to Chicago Ave., then turn east and walk 3 blocks to the house.

NEARBY
➤ Ernest Hemingway Museum and Birthplace, Oak Park
Conservatory.

COMMENT
➤ Plan a 2-hour visit. The neighborhood south of the Home and
Studio features numerous examples of Frank Lloyd Wright's work,
and fancy Victorian homes that you can see on foot.

The Immigrant Experience
JANE ADDAMS HULL
HOUSE MUSEUM

800 S. Halsted St., Chicago
(312) 413-5353
www.uic.edu/jaddams/hull/hull_house.html

C hicago is an immigrant city through and
through. Between the mid-19th and 20th centuries, millions of immigrants from countries
such as Sweden, Lithuania, Germany, China, Poland,
Italy and Greece to name a few, made Chicago their
home. The Jane Addams Hull House Museum honors
a woman who did much to make life comfortable for
these new arrivals. In the late 1880s, Addams created
and operated Hull House, a place where immigrants
could learn English and business skills, celebrate
holidays, play sports, and receive social services and
childcare. Thousands of new Americans benefited
from these services.

The museum occupies the original Hull
Mansion, which before the University of Illinois

expanded, sat in the middle of a bustling immigrant community. The museum experience begins with an informative 15-minute narrated slide show about Jane Addams and Hull House. Visitors can explore the mansion that is packed with pictures, books and other artifacts of the time. Young children simply enjoy examining the old rooms and furniture. Older children may be more interested in learning about the challenges their ancestors faced coming to a new country.

SEASONS AND TIMES
→ Year-round: Mon—Sat, 10 am—4 pm; Sun, noon—4 pm. Closed holidays.

COST
→ Free.

GETTING THERE
→ By car, take Adams St. west to Halsted St. Turn south and travel to the campus of the University of Illinois, Chicago. Hull House Museum is on the west side of Halsted in the middle of the campus. Pay parking garage across the street. About 15 minutes from Grant Park.
→ By public transit, take the Blue line El (towards Forest Park) to the UIC-Halsted stop. Walk south on Halsted to Hull House.

NEARBY
→ Maxwell Street Market, Sears Tower.

COMMENT
→ Plan a 30-minute visit. Family-friendly, ethnic restaurants are nearby. For outstanding Italian cuisine, head to the former Italian immigrant community (two blocks south on Halsted to Taylor St. and west a few blocks). Greektown is a few blocks north on Halsted.

The Sights, Sounds and Smells of
MAXWELL STREET MARKET

Near the corner of Canal St. and Roosevelt Rd., Chicago

The Maxwell Street Market was a huge open-air market where many immigrants got their start in business. The original market, which began operating in 1871, was torn down in 1994 to make way for the expanding University of Illinois. The "new" Maxwell Street Market, also open-air and located near the former site, is still a lot of fun to walk through. The history of the market lives on in the current vendors, who come from dozens of ethnic groups. You'll find them selling a huge assortment of goods, from exotic food products, to clothing and antiques, CDs and other flea market-type items. In good weather, blues bands provide incredible background music for the crowds. The sounds, smells and sights of the market make it a memorable Sunday jaunt, and you might find a bargain or two.

SEASONS AND TIMES
→ Year-round: Sun, 7 am—3 pm.

COST

➤ Free to browse.

GETTING THERE

➤ By car, take Roosevelt Rd. west to Clinton St. Turn south on Clinton and park in the lot ($3) behind the Dominick's Food Store. About 5 minutes from Grant Park.

➤ By public transit, take CTA bus 12 westbound on Roosevelt Rd. to the market.

NEARBY

➤ Jane Addams Hull House Museum.

COMMENT

➤ Maxwell Street Market is a great place for introducing children to the cultural diversity of Chicago. Plan a 2-hour visit.

Life in the 1800s
NAPER SETTLEMENT

523 S. Webster St., Naperville
(630) 420-6010
www.napersettlement.org

Instead of hearing about the good ol' days, children can live them at Naper Settlement. It's a 15-acre site that offers a glimpse into rural Illinois life in the 19th century. The village consists of historic buildings that were moved to the site from Naperville and surrounding communities. Actors dressed in period costume bring the village to life. They will be your guides, inviting you to explore the homes and shops while they perform day-to-day activities. Feel free to ask them questions. They may even ask you to help.

At the blacksmith shop, kids can see the blacksmith hammering out iron tools. At the firehouse, firemen might ask them to help hold down a hose that's spraying. A schoolhouse, a chapel, a print shop and several homes can also be visited. Anyone thrilled by military adventures will especially like the recreated fort. It was designed after Fort Payne, built in 1832 to protect the Naperville pioneers during the Blackhawk War.

The Visitor Center features a small but outstanding museum highlighting area history and a souvenir-packed general store. Special events, such as Civil War Days in May and Christmas Memories in December add to the fun!

SEASONS AND TIMES
➻ Apr—June: Tue—Sat, 10 am—4 pm; Sun, 1 pm—4 pm. July—Aug: Tue—Wed, 10 am—4 pm; Thu, 10 am—8 pm; Fri—Sat, 10 am—4 pm; Sun, 1 pm—4 pm. Sept—Oct: Tue—Sat, 10 am—4 pm; Sun, 1 pm—4 pm. Nov—Mar: Tue—Fri, 10 am—4 pm (actors not usually present and buildings are closed, but Visitor Center open and buildings can be viewed from the outside).

COST
➻ Summer: Adults $6.50, children (4 to 17) $4, under 4 free. Winter: Adults $3.25, children (4 to 17) $2, under 4 free.

GETTING THERE
➻ By car, take I-290 W. to I-88. Travel west on I-88 to the Naperville Rd. Exit. Turn right at the top of the ramp and travel south to Maple Ave. (also called Chicago Ave.) Turn west (right) on Maple and drive into downtown Naperville. Turn south (left) on Washington St. Travel 2 blocks to Porter Ave. and then turn west (right) and drive 2 blocks to Webster St. Free parking in the lot at the corner of Porter and Webster. About 50 minutes from Grant Park.

NEARBY
➤ Morton Arboretum, Cantigny Park.

COMMENT
➤ Plan a 3-hour visit—there's lots to see!

Old Chicago
PRAIRIE AVENUE
HISTORIC DISTRICT

Glessner House Museum, 1800 S. Prairie Ave., Chicago
(312) 326-1480
www.glessnerhouse.org

In the late 1800s, Prairie Avenue was Chicago's most elegant neighborhood. Retailer Marshall Field, meat packer Philip Armour and other famous people resided on this street in splendid mansions. When commercial development encroached on the area in the 1920s, many residents moved away. By 1960, most of the houses were demolished after land prices soared.

Fortunately, a few key homes survive along a one-block stretch of this famous street. Two of the houses are open for visits. It's a pleasant stroll through Chicago's late 19th-century history. Signs dotting a wrought iron fence recall the buildings that fell to the developer's wrecking ball.

The Glessner House Museum (at the north end of the block) was built in 1885 by John and Frances Glessner. This wealthy couple parted from traditional residential design to create this almost fortress-like house. Hour-long guided tours reveal its oak-paneled English Arts and Crafts design and furnishings. The Widow Clarke House, which faces Indiana Avenue but whose back yard is open to Prairie Avenue, also has tours. It was built in 1836 and is Chicago's oldest home.

Kids who like history will enjoy the tours and looking at the large homes on the street. Those under seven, however, may get bored. Take them for a romp through the Hillary Rodham Clinton Women's Park behind the Widow Clarke House.

SEASONS AND TIMES
➤ Tours (both houses): Year-round, Wed—Sun, noon—3 pm. Walking neighborhood tours: May—Sept, Sat. Call for times.

COST
➤ Tours (one house): Adults $7, children (5 to 12) $4, under 5 free. Tours (two houses): Adults $11, children (5 to 12) $7, under 5 free.

GETTING THERE
➤ By car, take Michigan Ave. south to 18th St. Turn east on 18th to Prairie Ave. Metered street parking. About 10 minutes from Grant Park.
➤ By public transit, take CTA buses 3 or 4 southbound on Michigan Ave. to 18th St. Walk 2 blocks east to Prairie Ave.

NEARBY
➤ The National Vietnam Veterans Art Museum (at the corner of 18th and Indiana) is 1 block west of Glessner House. Its depictions of the pain of warfare are a little intimidating for young kids, but mature teens may appreciate them.

COMMENT
➤ Plan a 1-hour visit.

Rocks of Ages
TRIBUNE TOWER

**435 N. Michigan Ave., Chicago
(312) 222-9100**

Tribune Tower is a 36-story skyscraper housing *The Chicago Tribune* newspaper. It's a beautiful structure built in 1922 in the gothic revival style, and acts as a gateway to North Michigan Avenue. What makes the building interesting are the stones embedded in the base of the tower. There are nearly 150 of them, each taken from famous structures or historic sites around the world. Go on a rock-finding expedition around the outside of the building and see how many of these treasures you can spot. Keep your eyes peeled for stones from the Taj Mahal, Westminster Abbey, the Parthenon and the Great Pyramids. All are identified.

The Chicago Tribune newsroom is not open to visits from the public, but you can watch a WGN radio broadcast. The studio is visible through a large window at street level on the Michigan Avenue side of the building. Inside, in the lobby, the *Tribune* gift shop sells *Tribune* T-shirts, miniature newspaper trucks and other such souvenirs.

SEASONS AND TIMES
➤ Gift shop: Year-round, Mon—Fri, 8 am—6 pm; Sat, 10 am—4 pm.

COST
➤ Free.

GETTING THERE
➤ By car, take Michigan Ave. north until you cross the Chicago River. The Tribune Tower is on the east side of the street. Pay lots in the neighborhood. About 5 minutes from Grant Park.
➤ By public transit, take any of the CTA buses that travel along Michigan Ave.

NEARBY
➤ Hancock Observatory, Chicago Water Tower, Magnificent Mile.

COMMENT
➤ Plan a 30-minute visit. Consider combining this with other nearby attractions. Gum-chewers in the family? Point out the Wrigley Building. It's across the street from the Tribune Tower.

Other Historical Sites

Pullman Historic District

11141 S. Cottage Grove Ave. (Pullman Visitor Center), Chicago • (773) 785-3828
http://members.aol.com/PullmanIL/visitor.html

Pullman was an important industrial town built by railroad car maker George Pullman in the 1880s. Learn about the history of the area at the Pullman Visitor Center and the nearby Hotel Florence. Guided walking tours of the area will interest all ages.

➤ Visitor Center: Year-round, Mon—Fri, noon—2 pm; Sat, 11 am—2 pm; Sun, noon—3 pm. Walking tours: First Sunday of the month, May—Oct, 12:30 pm and 1:30 pm.

➤Visitor Center: Adults $3, children $2. Tours: Adults $4, children $2.50.

➤ Take I-94 S. to the 111th St. Exit. Travel west on 111th to Cottage Grove Ave. and turn south. Street parking available. By public transit, take the Metra Electric Line from the Randolph St. Station to the Pullman Station (111th St.). The historic district is just east of the station.

Wrigley Field

Corner of Clark and Addison streets, Chicago
(773) 404-CUBS (2827)
www.cubs.com

Home to baseball's Chicago Cubs, Wrigley Field is a historic site and Major League ballpark rolled into one. The stadium was built in 1914 and originally housed the Chicago Whales franchise until the team folded. The Cubs moved into Wrigley Field in 1916 and have remained in the "friendly confines" ever since. Among its numerous distinctions, Wrigley Field was the site of Babe Ruth's famous "called shot" during the 1932 World Series, and more recently, one of the locations for the 1992 hit movie, *A League of Their Own*. Cubs' games are exciting to attend, but many fans just enjoy socializing, eating and basking in the fresh lake breezes that often blow into the stadium. Guided group tours of Wrigley Field are available and will take you behind the scenes. Call the number above or visit the website for details.

➤ The Cubs regular season runs from April through September. Call for game dates. Tours are held on select weekend dates during the season when the team is not playing at home.

➤ Games: Ticket prices range from $4 for children 13 and under (certain "value" games only) to $30. Regular prices for children start at $6. Adult ticket prices are $10 to $30. Tours cost from $10 to $15 per person.

➤ Take Lake Shore Dr. north to the Belmont Ave. Exit. Travel west on Belmont to Clark St. and go north on Clark to Addison St. Parking available in numerous small pay lots in the neighborhood. By public transit, take the Red line El to the Addison St. station. Walk 1 block west to the field.

CHAPTER 10

GETTING THERE IS HALF THE FUN

Introduction

Sometimes the trip is as entertaining as the destination. That is especially true for children who have never clip-clopped along the lakefront in a horse-drawn carriage, or bought a ticket and boarded the El. Chicago is a big city with many ways of getting around. Older kids get the thrill of a lifetime zipping along in a high-speed boat, while younger ones make believe they are pirates during a morning sail on Lake Michigan. A cushy chair on a double-decker Metra coach watching the world whiz by is the perfect place to see the scenery outside Chicago. A city tour on a trolley, pedaling a waterbike along a peaceful stretch of the Chicago River . . . pleasant diversions such as these make getting there part of the fun.

NOTE
You'll find these other fun ways to get there elsewhere in this guide:
Chicago River walk (Chapter 1, page 19)
Loop sculptures walking tour (Chapter 1, page 26)
Beach walks (Chapter 8, page 151)

Ride Like Royalty
J.C. CUTTERS CO.

**Corner of Chestnut St. and Michigan Ave., Chicago
(312) 644-6014
www.jccutters.com**

What could be more pleasant than clip-clopping along in a comfortable carriage pulled by a handsome steed? The notion sounds like a Dickens novel scene, but ride with J.C. Cutters and your family will tour Chicago in a luxurious horse-drawn carriage. It's fun, relaxing and an unusual way to see some of the Loop's most popular sights.

You'll be treated like royalty as your driver guides you through the downtown area, pointing out significant landmarks with commentary. The company has several different routes for your enjoyment. You decide whether it will be along the lakefront or into a shopping area. Each carriage holds four adults—more if the passengers are children—and contains cushy, upholstered seats. The carriages are convertible, meaning they are completely enclosed when the weather turns cold or wet. A big, warm blanket is provided and is perfect for bundling everyone up.

This slow, slightly bumpy ride is thoroughly enjoyable and will transport your family to an era when getting to get places didn't involve rushing.

SEASONS AND TIMES
➤ Year-round: Mon—Fri, 7 pm—1 am; Sat, 1 pm—2 am; Sun, 1 pm—1 am.

COST
➤ Each 30-minute ride costs $30 (regardless of the number of passengers). The drivers are paid on commission; tips are appreciated ($5 to $10 will suffice).

GETTING THERE
➤ By car, take Michigan Ave. north to Chestnut St. Parking is available in pay lots in the neighborhood. About 5 minutes from Grant Park.
➤ By public transit, take any CTA bus heading north on Michigan and get off at Chestnut.

NEARBY
➤ Water Tower, Magnificent Mile, Hancock Observatory.

COMMENT
➤ Everyone loves the ride, but children under 5 may get antsy after 10 to 15 minutes. Some drivers introduce and allow kids to pet the horses.

Exploring Chicago by
PUBLIC TRANSIT

**Chicago Transit Authority (CTA), Chicago
(312) 836-7000
www.yourcta.com**

C hicago's public transportation system makes it easy for tourists and residents alike to get to attractions around the city. Bus and El schedules can be obtained from the company's website. Or you can call the phone number listed above and receive detailed directions.

The El

For a memorable Chicago experience, ride the first car of the Loop-bound Brown line El during a snowstorm. You'll enjoy the wind whipped snow blowing by 100-year-old red brick buildings from the comfort of a cozy train. Even if you can't manage this, riding the El, or elevated railway, is a must-do activity when visiting Chicago.

Dating back to 1892, the El rumbles through the Loop, most Chicago neighborhoods and 38 surrounding suburbs. Commuters mainly use the El to travel to work, though riding it for the adventure can be a lot of fun as well. Kids especially love gazing out at the passing scenery, which can be quite fantastic. In most places, the train's elevated tracks are about three stories above the ground and within feet of the surrounding buildings. In the Loop, the train rolls along a "canyon" of skyscrapers. Elsewhere it travels in alleys behind residential brownstone flats, past smaller commercial areas and along busy highways. The most scenic El routes, such as the Brown line, circle the Loop and head north. You can board the Brown line at any Loop stop. To see the entire Loop, catch a train at the Washington or Quincy stops on the west side. If you're north of the river, board a Loop-bound train at Merchandise Mart.

The sights evaporate when the El goes underground, but that only heightens younger kids' excitement. Rush hour trains are standing-room only, but you might be lucky and find a group of empty seats.

City Buses

If you like to mingle with the locals, ride a CTA bus. You will encounter all types of passengers, from homeless folks riding around to stay warm, to business people traveling to work, to grandmothers heading to the market.

Chicago city buses can get you just about anywhere you need to go. Their routes are designed to fill the gaps between the El stops. However, be careful and don't hop on the first bus you see—some neighborhoods are safer for traveling than others. For a pleasant and scenic ride, take the 22 bus (Clark Street) from downtown. Catch it on Dearborn Street in the Loop, and ride it north through the Lincoln Park neighborhood and beyond.

SEASONS AND TIMES
➤ Year-round: Daily. Some Els and buses run continuously while others curtail service at night. Schedules are not always reliable, but are posted at each El stop. Train and bus service is less frequent on Sundays and holidays, but most operate. Call CTA or visit the website for details.

COST
➤ Bus or El (one-way): Adults $1.50, children (7 to 11) $0.75, under 7 free. Buses accept cash, fare cards or visitor passes. Els accept fare cards and passes. Remember to take a transfer card if you need one, as they cost less than paying two fares if you need to switch lines or buses (some restrictions apply). Fare cards start at $1.50 and are purchased from vending machines at El stations. They can be shared. Visitor passes start at $5 and come in 1- to 5-day increments. They are purchased at the O'Hare and Midway Airport CTA stations, Visitor Information Centers and some tourist attractions. They can also be ordered by phone and on-line.

COMMENT
➤ Officially only fold-up strollers are allowed on the El and children are not permitted to ride in them when the train is moving.

Passengers with larger strollers can ride in the disabled passenger's car—there is one on every train. Be prepared to make way for someone using a wheelchair. Only strollers that collapse completely can be carried onto a bus.

Riding in Style
CHICAGO TROLLEY CO.

4400 S. Racine Ave., Chicago (Administration)
(773) 648-5000
www.chicagotrolley.com

A t one time, streetcars regularly traveled Chicago streets. The Chicago Trolley Co. offers passengers the feeling of riding on one during its tour of the city. These trolleys don't run on tracks, but do feature solid oak and brass interiors. Your kids will agree they are a fun way to take in the sights.

Amiable guides provide an interesting commentary as you ride past popular downtown destinations. You will see the Sears Tower, Navy Pier, the Museum Campus and many other attractions along the 13-mile route. Why not take advantage of the company's "hop on, hop off service" and set your own pace? Buy a daily ticket and get off at any of the scheduled stops—then catch another trolley and continue the tour later. The trolleys are scheduled to go by each stop at 10- to 15-minute intervals.

In fine weather the cars are open-air, but enclosed and heated when required.

SEASONS AND TIMES
➤ Year-round: Daily, 9 am—6:30 pm (last guaranteed pick-up at each stop is 5 pm).

COST
➤ Daily ticket (unlimited rides): Adults $18, children (3 to 11) $8, under 3 free. One-Loop ticket (no re-boarding privilege): Adults $15, children (3 to 11) $8, under 3 free.

GETTING THERE
➤ You can buy tickets and board the trolley at any stop. Try the corner of Michigan Ave. and Wacker Dr., the Sears Tower or Navy Pier.

COMMENT
➤ One complete lap lasts about 1.5 hours.

Riding the Rails
METRA

Various stations in downtown Chicago
(312) 322-6777
www.metrarail.com

Metra is a fancier version of the El and is a commuter rail service that operates throughout northeastern Illinois. The system's 12 routes cover approximately 495 miles linking downtown Chicago with 230 stations in the counties of Cook, DuPage, Lake, Will, McHenry and Kane.

Whether your destination requires traveling 20 minutes or a couple of hours, riding a Metra train is a great way to take in the scenery surrounding Chicago. The cars feature all the accouterments of rail coach

travel with large comfortable seats and live con-
ductors moving about. A bonus for the kids is that the
trains are double-deckers and the view from the top
is excellent. Bicycles are not permitted on board the
trains. There are snack bars to satisfy hungry little
tummies.

SEASONS AND TIMES
➤ Year-round: Daily. Schedules vary, call Metra or visit its website for
details.

COST
➤ There are a variety of tickets available with fares assessed according
to the distance (or zones) traveled. Regular one-way fares for adults
range from $1.75 to $6.60, children (7 to 11) half price, under 7 free.
On weekends, youths (12 to 17) pay half price, under 12 ride free. A
good value is the $5 weekend pass that offers unlimited rides.

GETTING THERE
➤ There are several Metra stations in downtown Chicago. Included
are the Ogilvie Transportation Center on Washington St. between
Clinton St. and Canal St.; Union Station on Canal between Jackson
Blvd. and Adams St.; and a smaller station off Michigan Ave. between
Randolph St. and S. Water St.

Raise the Mainsail!
PIRATE ADVENTURE
CRUISE

Wagner Charter Co., Inc.
South bank of the Chicago River (at Wells St. Bridge),
Chicago
(800) 727-8926
www.wagnercharter.com

Here's a boat cruise everyone will be talking about long after it's over. The Pirate Adventure Cruise features a ride on the *Buccaneer*, a 100-foot vessel decorated with pirate trappings and flying the skull and crossbones. While parents take in the awesome views from the river and lakefront, kids eat up the pirate-theme entertainment. There's a wise-cracking pirate captain piloting the boat and a magician who puts on a clever show for all ages. Every sailor is given a free paper pirate hat and a soft drink. For kids who have ever dreamed of celebrating their birthdays at sea, the *Buccaneer* offers party packages.

SEASONS AND TIMES
→ Late Apr–mid-Oct: Sat, 10:30 am. Other days and times may be available. Call for information.

COST
→ Adults and children, $12. Reservations required.

GETTING THERE

➤ By car, take Van Buren St. or Adams St. west to Wells St. Turn north onto Wells and drive to Wacker Dr. There are pay parking lots in the vicinity. Walk down the stairs on the southwest corner of the Wells St. Bridge to the riverfront. The *Buccaneer* is docked on the south bank of the Chicago River across from Merchandise Mart. About 10 minutes from Grant Park.

COMMENT

➤ The cruise lasts 90 minutes.

Chicago by Water
BOAT CRUISES AND RIDES

C hicago, on Lake Michigan and with the Chicago River running through it, has options galore for seeing the sights from the water— from traditional cruises to waterbikes to high-powered speedboats.

RiverBikes
Chicago River at LaSalle St., Chicago
(888) RIVER11 (748-3711)
www.riverbikes.com

Get close to the Chicago River by riding a peddle-operated surfboard! A guide shows you how to operate your riverbike and points out the sites. Personal floatation devices are supplied.

➤ May—Oct: Daily, 10 am—dusk.

➤ Per person: $15 for 30 minutes.

➤ RiverBikes is located on the south bank of the Chicago River at LaSalle St.

Ugly Duck Cruises
Navy Pier, Chicago
(888) 741-0282
www.uglyduckcruises.com

Visitors to the waterfront can't miss the *Ugly Duck*. It's bright yellow! This big, beautiful boat plies the lake several times a day. On board, passengers can locate themselves on one of three decks—each features a brightly painted interior with tables offering unobstructed views of the lakefront and cityscape. A disc jockey entertains the crowd with music and games. Hors d'oeuvres or full meals are included.

↪ Year-round, less frequent in cold months. Daily schedules vary starting with a lunch cruise at 11:30 am and ending with a moonlight cruise at midnight. Cruises range from 1 1/2 hours to 3 hours duration.

↪ Prices vary, starting at $18 and going up to $55 per person. Food included. Reservations required.

↪ Take Lake Shore Dr. north to the Illinois Ave. Exit. Follow signs to Navy Pier, which is east of Lake Shore. Parking available in garages on the pier. By public transit, take CTA buses 29 (State St.) or 65 (Grand Ave.) to the pier's front entrance. A free trolley travels between Navy Pier and State St. Catch it beside the "Navy Pier Trolley Stop" signs. Take the lakefront path north or south directly to Navy Pier if biking or on foot.

Sea Dog
Navy Pier, Chicago
(312) 822-7200
www.uglyduckcruises.com

The same company that runs the *Ugly Duck* operates the *Sea Dog*—a much faster craft! This giant speed boat offers passengers exhilarating 30-minute rides along the lakefront and more tranquil 75-minute architectural tours along the Chicago River.

➤ Apr—Oct: Daily, multiple times throughout the day. Call for departure times.

➤ Mon—Thu: Adults $15, children (3 to 11) $10. Fri—Sat: Adults $16, children (3 to 11) $10.

➤ Take Lake Shore Dr. north to the Illinois Ave. Exit. Follow signs to Navy Pier, which is east of Lake Shore. Parking available in garages on the pier. By public transit, take CTA buses 29 (State St.) or 65 (Grand Ave.) to the pier's front entrance. A free trolley travels between Navy Pier and State St. Catch it beside the "Navy Pier Trolley Stop" signs. Take the lakefront path north or south directly to Navy Pier if biking or on foot.

Shoreline Sightseeing
Navy Pier, Shedd Aquarium and Buckingham Fountain, Chicago
(312) 222-9328
www.shorelinesightseeing.com

Shoreline operates cruises from three lakefront locations every half-hour. Narrators provide a primer on Chicago's landmarks and history while you take in the fantastic skyline views. Shoreline also operates the Water Taxi, which ferries passengers between various waterfront attractions, and the River Architecture Cruise.

➤ Sightseeing Cruise: May—Sept, daily departures from Navy Pier dock, Shedd Aquarium and Buckingham Fountain. Call for times. Water Taxi: Memorial Day—Labor Day, daily, 10 am—6 pm. Architectural Cruise: Apr and mid-Oct—Nov 30, Sat—Sun. May—mid-Oct, daily. Call for times.

➤ Sightseeing Cruise: Navy Pier dock, Adults $9, children (under 12) $4. Shedd Aquarium and Buckingham Fountain: Adults $8, children (under 12) $4. Water Taxi: Adults $6, children (under 12) $3. Architectural Cruise: Adults $15, children (under 12) $7.

➤ The Sightseeing Cruise leaves from Navy Pier, Shedd Aquarium and the lakefront in front of Buckingham Fountain. The Water Taxi operates between Navy Pier, Shedd Aquarium and the riverfront near Sears Tower (200 S. Wacker Dr.). The Architectural Cruise leaves from Navy Pier.

Wendella Boats
North end of the Michigan Ave. Bridge, Chicago
(312) 337-1446
www.wendellaboats.com

Wendella bills itself as Chicago's original narrated sightseeing ride and has been in operation since 1935. The company sails the waters of the Chicago River and Lake Michigan, passing all the points of interest along the way. Wendella also operates the *RiverBus*, a commuter boat that travels along the river with stops along the way.

➤ Wendella: Year-round, daily, 10 am—8:30 pm. Cruises vary from 1 to 2 hours. Fewer departures in colder weather. *RiverBus*: Apr—Nov, daily, usually 7:30 am—7:30 pm.

➤ Wendella tours (1-, 1 1/2- and 2-hour): Adults $12, $14 and $16; children (3 to 11) $6, $7 and $8, under 3 free. *RiverBus*: Adults and children $2.

➤ The Wendella docks just west of the north end of the Michigan Ave. Bridge. The *RiverBus* docks just north of the Madison Ave. Bridge with several stops up to Michigan Ave.

Mercury Cruise Line
South bank of Chicago River at Michigan Ave.
(312) 332-1353

Mercury offers three different narrated cruises along the Chicago River and the lakefront. All important sites are viewed.

➤ May 1—Oct 1: Daily. Landmark Classic: departs 10 am—8:30 pm. Summer Sunset Cruise: departs 7:30 pm. Skyline Special: departs 5 pm—9 pm.

➤ Prices: Adults $12 to $16, children (under 12) $6 to $8, varies by cruise.

➤ Boats dock on the south bank of the Chicago River at Michigan Ave. and Lower Wacker Dr.

Other Ways to See Chicago
WALK CHICAGO

Stretch your legs with a long stroll along the lake-front, or set your course through the Loop. Chicago offers extraordinary sights to walkers.

The lakefront path, running for 18 miles north and south of the Loop, goes past beaches, parks and other important attractions. In the spring or summer, enjoy the company of sunbathers, 'bladers, joggers and others out on the path. During winter, check out the amazing ice sculptures created by water spraying off the lake.

A walk in the Loop brings you past awesome public art, towering skyscrapers, beautiful architecture and all kinds of interesting people. Plan your outing to include sites bordered by Roosevelt Road on the south, the Chicago River on north and west, and Michigan Avenue on the east. Both routes only scratch the surface of great Chicago walks. Visit www.palmersguide.com/chicago for a list of others.

Remember to bring along a stroller if you have young ones. Snacks and liquids are also walking essentials when you're with kids. Catch a ride back to your home or hotel using Chicago's public transportation if you wander too far.

➤ Year-round. Daily.

➤ Free.

➤ Access the lakefront by heading east through Grant Park, across Lake Shore Dr.

Bike Chicago
Navy Pier and North Ave. Beach, Chicago
(800) 915-2453
www.bikechicago.com
www.cityofchicago.org/Transportation/Bikes

Chicago is an awesome city to tour by bicycle. Traversing downtown streets may be a bit too daring for young riders, but wonderful scenery awaits families in city parks and along the lakefront.

Bike Chicago on Navy Pier (and at the boathouse on North Avenue Beach) has bike rentals—from bikes for kids to chunky wheeled off-road two-wheelers to quadcycles for families. Pick up a free map at Bike Chicago and enjoy one of five tours featuring popular routes along the lakefront. Or, join one of the free tours that leave every day at 11:30 am going to either Lincoln Park Zoo or Hyde Park. The tour to Lincoln Park Zoo takes a little over two hours. The ride to Hyde Park is about four hours. You can bring your own bikes and still go on these tours. Bike Chicago also rents in-line skates.

For more information on bike riding in Chicago, check out the Department of Transportation's website above.

➤ Apr—Oct: Mon—Sun, 8 am—8 pm.

➤ Bicycle and in-line skates: $5 to $9 per hour. Quadcycles: $20 per hour (small), $25 (large). Daily and weekly rates. Helmets included in the rental.

➤ Navy Pier location: Take Lake Shore Dr. north to the Illinois Ave. Exit. Follow signs to Navy Pier, which is east of Lake Shore. Parking available in garages on the pier. By public transit, take the CTA bus 29 (State St.) or 65 (Grand Ave.) to the pier's front entrance. A free trolley travels between Navy Pier and State St. Catch it beside "Navy Pier Trolley Stop" signs. North Ave. Beach location: Take Lake Shore Dr. to the North Ave. Exit. Park in lot or in underground garage at corner of North and Clark St.

CHAPTER 11

FAVORITE
FESTIVALS

Introduction

C hicago loves its festivals! From neighborhood street fairs to the big extravaganzas in
the Loop, area residents can't get enough of
the food, music and fun that festivals bring.
Summer is prime festival time, with the Taste of
Chicago leading the way. Smaller parties, such the
Andersonville Midsommarfest and the Taste of
Lincoln Avenue, provide much of the same flavor
only without the crowds! The Chicago Folk & Roots
Festival will get your children's feet moving. If you
love speed, then the Chicago Air & Water Show with
its blast of action along North Avenue Beach is the
place for you to be.

Fall and winter are festival-full, too. The
Chicago International Children's Film Festival is a
must-see for cinema fans. The city comes alive
around Christmas with parades down State Street
and Michigan Avenue. For even more festivals, go
to the Directory of Events at the back of this book.
Enjoy!

Everyone's Irish Today
ST. PATRICK'S DAY PARADE

**Along Dearborn St.,
from Wacker Dr. to Van Buren St., Chicago**

This annual celebration of Chicago-Irish heritage is a fun, though often chilly, early-spring adventure. The parade, which is mostly a display of community pride, features herds of politicians, police officers, fire fighters, union organizations and other groups marching en masse through the Loop. Kids always enjoy seeing the bagpipe bands, sponsored by various city and community groups, and the marching bands from area high schools. Multiple troupes of Irish step dancers and floats round out the procession.

Perhaps the signature event of the festivities is the dying of the Chicago River. To do this a small boat winds down the river, spilling green dye into the water to color it a bright, lime green. It's a sight to be seen!

On the same weekend a second, smaller parade proceeds along Western Avenue from 103rd to 115th streets in the Irish-American neighborhood on the South Side.

SEASONS AND TIMES

➤ The downtown parade takes place the Saturday closest to St. Patrick's Day (March 17). The South Side parade is held the next day.

COST

➤ Free.

GETTING THERE

➤ By car, take Van Buren St. or Adams St. east to Dearborn St. Park in one of the pay lots along the way. About 5 minutes from Grant Park.
➤ By public transit, take the El and get off at any one of the stops in the Loop.

NEARBY

➤ Art Institute, Spertus Museum, Sears Tower, Grant Park.

COMMENT

➤ Wear warm clothes and get there early to stake out a good spot. This parade is mostly about people watching, so kids 5 and under will probably get bored quickly.

Mexican Pride
FESTIVAL CINCO DE MAYO

**McCormick Place, Chicago
(312) 751-5560**

Cinco de Mayo (translated the Fifth of May) marks Mexico's defeat of the French army at The Battle of Puebla in 1862. It was a significant victory for a ragtag Mexican militia, but Napoleon promptly dispatched a much larger force and eventually won the war. Nevertheless, Cinco de

Mayo is proudly celebrated in parts of Mexico and in American cities with large Mexican populations, such as Chicago.

Chicago's celebration is centered in McCormick Place, where Mexican-Americans and others mingle in a party-like atmosphere for a weekend of family-oriented fun and festivities. You can sample expertly prepared, authentic Mexican cuisine, listen to lively mariachis, view Mexican art and soak up the ethnic atmosphere that is such an important part of this city.

SEASONS AND TIMES
➤ Generally the weekend before May 5. Call for exact dates and times.

COST
➤ Individuals $10, under 12 free.

GETTING THERE
➤ By car, take Lake Shore Dr. south. McCormick Place will be on the east side as soon as you pass Soldier Field. Follow signs to pay parking lots around McCormick Place. About 10 minutes from Grant Park.
➤ By public transit, take CTA buses 3 or 4 along Michigan Ave. to McCormick Place.

NEARBY
➤ Field Museum, Adler Planetarium, Shedd Aquarium.

COMMENT
➤ Mexican restaurants throughout Chicago hold their own parties marking Cinco de Mayo.

Dancing in the Streets NEIGHBORHOOD FESTIVALS

www.ci.chi.il.us/SpecialEvents

Chicago is known as the city of neighborhoods. Each celebrates its own distinctive character during their annual festivals. The recipe for good times is the same as the major festivals: tasty food, music, arts and crafts and lots of socializing in the street. Attending is a fun and inexpensive way to experience the Chicago that is beyond the city's more touristy attractions.

The Mayor's Office of Special Events website (listed above) has a comprehensive list of street fairs and dates. Here are some of the popular ones—all are definitely worth checking out.

Andersonville Midsommarfest

On Clark St. (from Foster Ave. to Balmoral Ave.), Chicago
(773) 728-2995

Andersonville is a neighborhood on Chicago's Far North Side that was once home to thousands of Scandinavian immigrants. It retains its ethnic flavor through its shops and restaurants. Heritage and summer are celebrated during the Andersonville Midsommarfest, a street party that features ethnic dance troupes, live bands and over 80 artists displaying their wares.

➛ Early June. Call for exact dates and times.

➤ Take Lake Shore Dr. north to the Foster Ave. Exit. Travel west on Foster to Clark St. Limited street parking available. About 30 minutes from Grant Park. By public transit, take the Red line El to the Berwyn stop. Walk 1 block south to Foster, then 6 blocks west to Clark.

Chinatown Summer Fair and Chinese New Year Parade
On Wentworth St. (from Cermak Rd. to 24th St.), Chicago
(773) 225-6198

Walk through Chinatown and you will swear you are in the Orient. The commercial signs are mostly in Chinese, the stores and restaurants offer an array of exotic goods and food, and many of the faces, from young children to grandparents, are distinctly Asian. Chinatown is a fascinating place for kids to visit any time of year. The Summer Fair and the New Year Parade offer an especially colorful blast of Chinese culture. There are delicious authentic foods, colorful costumes, firecrackers and traditional and contemporary music.

➤ The Summer Fair is held in mid-July. The New Year Parade is in February. Call for exact dates and times.

➤ Take State St. south from the Loop to Cermak Rd. Turn west on Cermak and drive to Chinatown. Pay lots and metered street parking are available in the area. About 15 minutes from Grant Park.

Taste of Lincoln Avenue
Lincoln Ave. (from Fullerton Ave. to Wrightwood St.), Chicago
(773) 472-9046

The Taste features much the same menu as the bigger Taste of Chicago downtown, except you have the advantage of ogling the prosperous north side neighborhood between courses. The highlight for the younger festival-goers is the block-long Kid's Karnival with clowns, jugglers, games and a petting zoo.

➤ Mid-July. Call for exact dates and times.

➤ Take Lake Shore Dr. north to the Fullerton Ave. Exit. Travel west on Fullerton to Lincoln Ave. Limited street parking is available. About 15 minutes from Grant Park. By public transit, take the El (Brown or Red lines) to the Fullerton Ave. stop. Walk east for 3 blocks to Lincoln.

Finger Lickin' Good!
TASTE OF CHICAGO

Grant Park (bounded by Michigan Ave., Lake Shore Dr., Randolph St. and Roosevelt Rd.), Chicago
(312) 744-3370
www.cityofchicago.org/SpecialEvents/Festivals.html

The Taste of Chicago is a popular event on the family festival calendar where visitors get a triple dose of pure Chicago. You can sample some of the best food in town in beautiful Grant Park amid lots of toe-tapping music and other live entertainment.

This annual happening takes place from late June until shortly after Independence Day and features over 100 Chicago restaurants offering samples of their finest goods. Try lip-smacking barbecued ribs or turkey legs, giant slices of stuffed pizza, crispy vegetable tempura or any of the other tasty delectables. Top it off with an ice cream cone and you have the perfect, open-air summer lunch!

There is great music too. On several stages in the park are local and national acts performing blues, rock, country and other types of music. For a special treat, visit Grant Park on the 3rd of July (you will have to squeeze in with thousands of other revelers) to enjoy the Chicago Symphony Orchestra perform in the Petrillo Band shell. The concert is accompanied by an extraordinary fireworks show.

SEASONS AND TIMES
➤ Late June—early July: Daily, 11 am—9 pm. Call for exact dates.

COST
➤ Admission is free. Food tickets must be purchased and are available at booths in the park and at some local grocery stores. One entrée and a beverage average 10 tickets ($6).

GETTING THERE
➤ By car, take Lake Shore Dr. or Michigan Ave. to Jackson St., Monroe St. or Balbo St. All cut through Grant Park. Pay parking available at underground garages at the corners of Monroe and Columbus Ave., Michigan and Van Buren St., Michigan and Monroe, as well as on the street.
➤ By public transit, take any of the CTA buses that run along Michigan to Grant Park. Take any of the El lines that circle the Loop and get off at Adams St. or Madison St. and walk east to the park.
➤ By bicycle, follow the lakefront path.

NEARBY
➤ The Art Institute of Chicago, Spertus Museum, Field Museum, Adler Planetarium, Shedd Aquarium.

COMMENT
➤ The Taste gets crowded during weekends and evenings. Try for a weekday lunch if your schedule allows.

Stomp Your Feet
CHICAGO FOLK
& ROOTS FESTIVAL

**Welles Park (corner of Lincoln
and Montrose avenues), Chicago
(773) 728-6000**

This weekend-long feast of music and dance is sure to get your kids swaying to the rhythm. For little ones the best part is the Kids' Tent, which features the ever-changing mix of dance, music and storytelling. In the past, Kids' Tent has included a Barn Dance, a Musical Theater and an Improv Hour.

While youngsters are yukking it up in their tent, you can visit the Dance and Workshop Tent to learn the two-step, the polka or just sing along with a folk group. The Main Stage regularly features well known folk acts the whole family can enjoy. Entertainers such as Patti Smith have previously headlined here.

The Old Town School of Folk Music, whose main building is located on Lincoln Avenue just north of Welles Park, operates the festival. Read about its offerings for kids on page 124 of this book.

SEASONS AND TIMES
➤ One weekend in mid-July: Noon—9 pm (or when the last act finishes). Call for exact dates.

COST
➤ Suggested donation: Adults $5, children $1.

GETTING THERE
➤ By car, take I-90/94 north to the Western Ave. Exit. Travel north on Western to Welles Park, which is bound by Western, Montrose Ave., Sunnyside Ave. and Lincoln Ave. Note: travel by car is not recommended owing to the extremely limited street parking. About 30 minutes from Grant Park.
➤ By public transit, take the Brown line El to the Western Ave. stop. Walk south on Western for 2 blocks to Welles Park.

NEARBY
➤ Old Town School of Folk Music.

COMMENT
➤ Walk 1/2 mile north of Welles Park on Lincoln Ave. and you will come to Lincoln Square. This quaint neighborhood was settled by German immigrants and has an old European flavor with several German delis, restaurants and stores.

High-flying Fun
CHICAGO AIR & WATER SHOW

North Ave. Beach, Chicago
www.cityofchicago.org/SpecialEvents/Festivals.html

Zooming planes and roaring speedboats are simply downright fun to watch. The Chicago Air & Water Show offers spectators plenty of both, with the beach being the best place to do it.

The water show features every kind of speed boat imaginable in races and in exhibitions—cover your ears, they are extremely loud. But it is the air show that draws the crowds. Regular participants include the U.S. Navy Blue Angels, considered by many to be the ultimate air acrobatic troupe. Their ultra high-speed maneuvers and coordinated jet streams are awe-inspiring. Each year the Blue Angels are joined by a gaggle of other interesting acts, including stunt pilots and precision flyers.

Fighting the crowds will be your biggest challenge. The show is performed along North Avenue Beach, which is packed even on regular summer weekends. However, the aircraft show can be viewed from just about anywhere on the lakefront, from the Museum Campus to Montrose Harbor. Come early and stake out your spot in the sand to take full advantage of the festivities. Vendors set up along the lakefront path will keep you fed and hydrated.

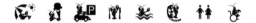

SEASONS AND TIMES
→ One weekend in mid-August. The water show starts at 10 am and the air show at noon. Call for exact dates and times.

COST
→ Free.

GETTING THERE
→ By car, take Lake Shore Dr. north to the North Ave. Exit. Park in the metered lot at the beach, or travel west to the pay garage at the corner of North and Clark St. Alternatively, stay on Lake Shore and take the Fullerton Ave. Exit and travel west to the Lincoln Park Zoo pay lot (at Fullerton and Cannon Dr.). About 15 minutes from Grant Park. Note: if you plan to drive, arrive early as people start staking out prime spots on the beach as early as 6 am.
→ By public transit, take CTA bus 151 on Michigan Ave. and ride it to North. Walk east to the beach. Or take the El (Brown or Red lines) to the Belmont or Fullerton Ave. stop, then walk east to the beach. It's a hike from either stop, so do not bring along more than you can comfortably carry.

➝ By bike or on foot, take the lakefront path north to North Ave. Beach.

NEARBY
➝ Lincoln Park Zoo, Peggy Notebaert Nature Center.

COMMENT
➝ Bring sunscreen, beverages and a blanket to spread on the sand. If you drive, consider staying at the beach after the show (to avoid the traffic) and make a day of it.

Ready on the Set!
CHICAGO INTERNATIONAL CHILDREN'S FILM FESTIVAL

Facets Multimedia, 1517 W. Fullerton Ave., Chicago
(773) 281-9075
www.cicff.org

Kids love going to the movies, right? Well, there is no better way to indulge them than at the Chicago International Children's Film Festival. This annual event, held over ten days, features upwards of 180 movies from around the world (all new releases) that are appropriate for children between the ages of 2 and 15. A jury of adults and children selects the films for their quality and humanistic values. Recent presentations have included *I'll Remember April* starring Haley Joel Osment and *The Spooky House* with Ben Kingsley.

You can watch the movies at two locations: Facets Multimedia, the organization that runs the festival, and General Cinemas' new outlet at 2600 North Western Avenue. It has stadium seating and state-of-the-art sound and projection.

The festival also gives kids the hands-on chance to learn how to make their own films. Take One! Workshops is a series of classes taught by experienced filmmakers that introduces children to movie-making and careers in the business (reservations are required).

SEASONS AND TIMES
➤ Mid to late October. Screening times vary. Call the festival or visit its website for schedule information.

COST
➤ $6 per person, per film. Prices for Take One! Workshops range from $15 to $30.

GETTING THERE
Facets Multimedia:
➤ By car, take I-90/94 west to the Armitage Ave. Exit. Travel east on Armitage to Ashland Ave. and turn north. Continue on Ashland to Fullerton Ave. and turn east. Facets Multimedia is on the south side of Fullerton. Look for free street parking on the side streets. About 15 minutes from Grant Park.
➤ By public transit, take the El (Brown or Red lines) to the Fullerton stop, then walk west for 4 blocks.
General Cinema:
➤ By car, take I-90/94 west to the Western Ave. Exit. Travel north on Western to General Cinema. It is on the west side of the street. The on-site pay lot charges $2 if you have your ticket validated in the theater. About 15 minutes from Grant Park.

COMMENT
Depending on your kids' ages, one movie per day is probably enough.

Ring in the Season!
FIELD'S JINGLE ELF PARADE

**From Congress Pkwy. and State St. proceeding north
to Randolph St., Chicago
www.chicagofestivals.org**

C hicago loves Christmas, and nothing kicks off the season better than the Jingle Elf Parade on Thanksgiving Day. Hundreds of thousands of spectators line the parade route every year to watch colorful floats, marching bands and giant helium-inflated figures go filing past.

This much-anticipated holiday parade dates back to 1934 when the Greater State Street Council came up with the idea for having a parade as a way to stimulate holiday sales during the Depression. It has been held every year since.

Come early to get a good curbside viewing spot. After the parade, plan to take your family to see the elaborate holiday displays in the windows on Marshall Fields' State Street store (111 N. State St.) and Carson Pirie Scott (1 S. State St.). They are magical.

SEASONS AND TIMES
➤ Thanksgiving Day. Parade begins at 8:30 am.

COST
➤ Free.

GETTING THERE

➤ State St. is the heart of the Loop. If you plan on driving, arrive well before 8:3o am. Access along the parade route is closed in advance and traffic becomes congested throughout the Loop. Pay parking is available in multiple garages and lots near State. Minutes from Grant Park.

➤ By public transit, take any El line heading towards the Loop. Get off at any stop on the east side of the Loop.

NEARBY

➤ Grant Park, Art Institute.

COMMENT

➤ Dress warmly. The wind can really whip down the "canyons" created by the Loop's tall buildings.

Holiday Fun, Mag Mile Style
MAGNIFICENT MILE
LIGHTS FESTIVAL

**Parade (Oak St. north on Michigan Ave. to Wacker Dr.);
Stage Shows (in Pioneer Court on Michigan Ave.,
just north of the Chicago River), Chicago
(312) 409-5560
www.lightsfestival.com**

Not wanting to be left out of the holiday fun, Michigan Avenue hosts its own parade and festivities a week before the famous parade on State Street. Walt Disney World Resort brings added kid appeal to this one.

The Magnificent Mile Lights Festival features three stage shows with Disney characters guaranteed to delight the younger set. Mickey Mouse is always the star attraction, but Goofy, Pluto and the other Disney favorites, plus a handsome troupe of energetic human singers and dancers bring real gusto to the show. It is a small taste of Disney magic right in downtown Chicago.

On Saturday evening, Mickey leads the parade down Michigan Avenue. Block by block he waves his magic wand to light the one million-plus bulbs strung in the trees lining the street. Cinderella, Belle and the Beast, Prince Charming and other Disney characters join the famous mouse in the procession. As if the parade and shows alone won't fire a youngster's excitement, there is also a petting zoo with Santa's reindeer and a life-size gingerbread house.

SEASONS AND TIMES
→ The Saturday before Thanksgiving. The stage shows take place at 11 am, 1 and 3 pm. The parade starts at 6 pm.

COST
→ Free.

GETTING THERE
→ By car, take Michigan Ave. north until you cross the bridge over the Chicago River. Pay parking is available in several pay lots and garages off the side streets. About 5 minutes from Grant Park.
→ By public transit, take the Red line El to the Grand Ave. stop. Walk east to Michigan Ave. Or take any of the CTA buses that travel along Michigan.

NEARBY
→ Navy Pier, Chicago River, Hancock Observatory.

COMMENT
→ Get there early to find a spot on the curb. Crowds form deep lines along the parade route.

Room & Board

KID-FRIENDLY RESTAURANTS

Eating out with the family offers numerous rewards, chief among them is that someone else does the cooking. Luckily, there is no shortage of restaurants in Chicago and surrounding areas that offer families a fun atmosphere, good food at reasonable prices and friendly staff. Better still, most of the restaurants listed below offer kids' menus or kid-sized portions upon request, booster and high chairs, crayons and paper to keep little hands occupied. Many accommodate nursing moms and provide baby changing stations.

Chicago is a city of wholesome cooking and hearty portions, famous for its delicious ribs, pizza and Italian beef. But Chicago's gourmet cuisine doesn't stop there, so round up the troops and don't miss out on the wide variety of tasty vittles found at eateries around the city.

Ann Sather's Restaurant

(Delicious breakfasts, kid-friendly staff)
3416 N. Southport Ave., Chicago (773) 404-4475
2665 N. Clark St., Chicago (773) 327-9522
5207 N. Clark St., Chicago (773) 271-6677
929 W. Belmont Ave. Chicago (773) 348-2378
3411 N. Broadway St., Chicago (773) 305-0024

Brother Jimmy's Barbecue
(Great ribs and generous side dishes; kids' menu; fun
Southern atmosphere)
2909 N. Sheffield Ave., Chicago (773) 528-0888

Bubba Gump Shrimp Co.
(Seafood in a fun, lively atmosphere; great smoothies)
Navy Pier, Chicago (312) 595-5500

Café Luigi
(Awesome pizza by the slice; calzones; Italian
specialties; inexpensive)
2548 N. Clark St., Chicago (773) 404-0200

Carm's Beef and Italian Ice
(Excellent beef sandwiches; fast service; inexpensive)
1057 W. Polk St., Chicago (312) 738-1046

Chicago Brauhaus
(Authentic German cuisine in a fun, family-friendly
atmosphere)
4732 N. Lincoln Ave., Chicago (773) 784-4444

Ed Debevics Short Order
(1950s decor; great burgers, onion rings, friendly staff)
640 N. Wells St., Chicago (312) 664-1707

Erik's Deli
(Family-friendly; lots of room; boosters)
107 N. Oak Park Ave., Oak Park (708) 848-8805

Foodlife
(Food court with tons of healthy choices; great for
picky kids)
Water Tower Place, 835 N. Michigan Ave., Chicago
(312) 335-3663

Giordano's
(Great stuffed pizza; kid-friendly staff; boosters)
1040 W. Belmont Ave., Chicago (773) 327-1200
5927 W. Irving Park Rd., Chicago (773) 736-5553
9613 S. Western Ave., Chicago (773) 445-6255
130 E. Randolph St., Chicago (312) 616-1200
310 W. Randolph St., Chicago (312) 201-1441
815 W. Van Buren St., Chicago (312) 421-1221
730 N. Rush St., Chicago (312) 951-0747
5311 S. Blackstone Ave., Chicago (773) 947-0200
28 E. Jackson Blvd., Chicago (312) 939-4646

Gold Coast Dogs
(Genuine "Chicago dogs"; great burgers and cheddar fries)
418 N. State St., Chicago (312) 527-1222
225 S. Canal St., Chicago (312) 258-8585
2 N. Riverside Dr., Chicago (312) 879-0447
159 N. Wabash Ave., Chicago (312) 917-1677

Las Fuentes
(Mexican food; friendly staff; colorful, fun decor)
2558 N. Halsted, Chicago (773) 935-2004

Leona's Restaurant
(Good pizza, pasta; most locations have party/game rooms)
3215 N. Sheffield Ave., Chicago (773) 327-8861
3877 N. Elston Ave., Chicago (773) 267-7287
1236 E. 53rd St., Chicago (773) 363-2600
6935 N. Sheridan Rd., Chicago (773) 764-5757
7443 W. Irving Park Rd., Chicago (773) 625-3636
11060 S. Western Ave., Chicago (773) 881-7700
1419 W. Taylor St., Chicago (312) 850-2222
2501 S. Western Ave., Chicago (773) 523-7497
1936 W. Augusta Blvd., Chicago (773) 292-4300

The Parthenon
(Greek food; kids items on menu; family-friendly)
314 S. Halsted St., Chicago (312) 726-2407

Penny's Noodle Shop

(Inexpensive; noodles and other Asian dishes)
950 W. Diversey Pkwy., Chicago (773) 281-8448
3400 N. Sheffield Ave., Chicago (773) 281-8222

Potbelly Sandwich Works

(The best sub in Chicago; friendly service; fun decor)
758 W. North Ave., Chicago (312) 768-2355
190 N. State St., Chicago (312) 683-1234
2264 N. Lincoln Ave., Chicago (773) 528-1405
1422 W. Webster Ave., Chicago (773) 755-1234

Rainforest Café

(Jungle theme; animatronic animals; kids' menu;
birthdays; gift shop)
605 N. Clark St., Chicago (312) 787-1501

R.J. Grunts

(Fun 1960s decor; hearty food)
2056 N. Lincoln Park W., Chicago (773) 929-5363

Russell's Barbeque

(Kids' menu; kids get toys)
1621 N. Thatcher Ave., Elmwood Park (708) 453-7065

Salt & Pepper Diner

(Authentic diner; great breakfast food)
2575 N. Lincoln Ave., Chicago (773) 525-8788
3537 N. Clark St., Chicago (773) 883-9800

FAMILY-FRIENDLY HOTELS

Looking for home-away-from-home comfort when you are on vacation? Face it, staying at a hotel can be hectic when you're traveling as a family. New surroundings, an unfamiliar bed—it can unsettle even the most adventurous child. Whether your stay in Chicago is a few days or a couple of weeks, the family-friendly establishments below will make sure your brood wakes up refreshed and ready to take on a new day.

In addition to providing a relaxed atmosphere, most have services for families, from babysitting and kids' clubs to games rooms and more. Some of these hotels offer family discounts, too—a good thing considering you are on vacation.

Best Western Inn of Chicago
(Under 18 stay free; near Magnificient Mile)
162 E. Ohio St., Chicago (312) 787-3100

City Suites Hotel
(Near Lincoln Park)
933 W. Belmont Ave., Chicago (773) 404-3400

Congress Plaza Hotel
(Under 17 stay free; video game room; near Grant Park)
520 S. Michigan Ave., Chicago (312) 427-3800

Days Inn Lake Shore Hotel
(near beach and Navy Pier)
644 N. Lakeshore Dr., Chicago (312) 943-9200

Doubletree Guest Suites
(under 18 stay free; indoor pool)
198 E. Delaware Pl., Chicago (312) 664-1100

Holiday Inn City Center

(Under 18 stay free; two pools; Nintendo™)
300 E. Ohio St., Chicago (312) 787-6100

Palmer House Hilton

(Under 18 stay free; Indoor pool; pets allowed)
17 E. Monroe St., Chicago (312) 726-7500

Quality Inn Downtown

(Under 18 stay free; Inexpensive; near Greektown and
Sears Tower)
Madison at Halsted, Chicago (312) 829-5000

Sheraton Chicago Hotel & Towers

(Under 12 stay free; Indoor pool; near Navy Pier)
301 E. North Water St., Chicago (877) 242-2558

Wyndham Downtown

(Under 18 stay free; indoor pool)
633 N. St. Clair, Chicago (312) 573-0300

12 Months of Fun
DIRECTORY OF EVENTS

JANUARY
Late January
Jazz Fair
Chicago Cultural Center
(312) 427-1676

Late January
Chinese New Year Parade
Chinatown
(312) 225-6198

FEBRUARY
Early February
Chicago Cubs Convention
Loop
(773) 404-CUBS

Early February
Chicago White Sox Soxfest
Loop
(312) 565-0769

Mid-February
WinterFest
Morton Arboretum
(630) 968-0074

MARCH
Mid-March
Chicago Flower & Garden Show
Navy Pier
(312) 321-0077

Mid-March
St. Patrick's Day Parade
State St.
(312) 421-1010

APRIL
Late April
Antiques & Garden Fair
Chicago Botanic Garden
(847) 835-5440

Late April
Festival Cinco de Mayo
McCormick Place
(312) 751-5560

MAY
Early May
Mayor Daley's Kids & Kites Fest
Montrose Harbor
(312) 744-3370

Mid-May
Civil War Days
Naper Settlement, Naperville
(630) 305-5555

Late May
Memorial Day Parade
Chicago
(312) 269-7930

JUNE
Early June
Winnetka Children's Fair
Winnetka Village Green,
Winnetka
(847) 446-4432

Early June
Andersonville Midsommarfest
North Side
(773) 728-2995

Early June
Frontier Fest
Palos Park Children's Farm
(708) 361-3650

Early June
Elmfest
Downtown Elmhurst
(630) 834-6060

Early June
Summerfest
Madison Ave., Forest Park
(708) 366-2543

Early June
Kids Expo
Darien Community Park,
Darien
(630) 655-6400

Early June to August
Ravinia Kraft Kids Concerts
Series
Ravinia Park, Highland Park
(847) 266-5100

Mid-June
Greater Chicago Jewish Folk
Arts Festival
Caldwell Woods Forest Preserve
(847) 933-3000

Mid-June
Chicago Highland Games &
Scottish Festival
Oak Brook Polo Grounds
(708) 442-7293

Mid-June
Puppetropolis Chicago Puppet
Festival
Various locations throughout
Chicago
(312) 744-4405

Late June
Family Heritage Days
Naper Settlement, Naperville
(630) 305-5555

Late June
Family Fest
Bloomingdale
(630) 893-7000

Late June
Kids' Fest
Village Green Gazebo,
Northbrook
(847) 291-2960

Late June to early July
Taste of Chicago/4th of July
Celebration
Grant Park
(312) 744-3370

JULY
Early July
Waukegan Heritage Festival
Bowen Park, Waukegan
(847) 360-4762

Early July
Children's Arts Fair
Cuneo Museum and Gardens,
Vernon Hills
(847) 362-3042

Mid-July
Mayor's Cup Youth Soccer Fest
Lakefront
(312) 744-3370

Mid-July
Chinatown Summer Fair
Chinatown
(773) 225-6198

Mid-July
Dearborn Garden Walk and
Heritage Festival
Gold Coast area
(773) 472-6561

Late July
Venetian Night
Along the Lakefront
(312) 744-3370

Late July
Sheffield Garden Walk and
Festival
Sheffield Ave.
(773) 929-9255

Late July
Country Farm Fair
Maine Park, Park Ridge
(847) 692-5127

Late July
Kids Fest
Northbrook
(847) 291-2980

Late July
Summer Festival
Hoosier Grove Park,
Streamwood
(630) 837-0200

Late July
Corn Boil Festival
Sugar Grove
(630) 466-5166

AUGUST
August
Chicago Outdoor Film Festival
Grant Park
(312) 744-3370

Early August
Lake Forest Days
West Park, Lake Forest
(847) 234-2332

Early August
McHenry County Fair
Woodstock
(815) 338-5315

Early August
Fox Rox Festival
Downtown St. Charles
(630) 513-5386

Early August
Lake County Folk Festival
Lake Zurich
(847) 540-5527

Mid-August
Summerfest
Bartlett
(630) 830-0324

Mid-August
Gurnee Days
Viking Park, Gurnee
(847) 249-5596

Mid-August
Grayslake Summer Days
Grayslake
(847) 223-6888

Mid-August
Korean Street Festival
Bryn Mawr Ave.
(773) 583-1700

Late August
Trolleyfest
Fox Valley Trolley Museum,
South Elgin
(847) 697-4676

Late August
Tall Ships Chicago
Navy Pier
(312) 595-PIER

Late August
Chicago Jazz Festival
Grant Park
(312) 744-3370

Late August
Bucktown Arts Fest
Memorial Park
(312) 409-8305

Late August
Summerfest
Wood Dale
(630) 350-8300

Late August
Family Fun Festival
Des Plaines
(847) 391-5700

Late August
Celebrating South Shore
Festival
Jeffrey Plaza and Rosenblum
Park
(773) 324-0494

Late August
Arlington Heights County Fair
Arlington Heights Historical
Museum
(847) 255-1225

Late August
Buffalo Grove Days
Buffalo Grove
(847) 459-2500

SEPTEMBER
Early September
African Festival of the Arts
Washington Park
(773) 955-ARTS

Mid-September
An Old Fashioned Circus
Naper Settlement
(630) 305-5555

Mid-September
Celtic Fest Chicago
Grant Park
(312) 744-3370

Late September
Black Expo Chicago
McCormick Place
(773) 873-9440

OCTOBER
Late October
Chicagoween Fest
Various locations
(312) 744-3370

Late October
Spooky Zoo Spectacular
Lincoln Park Zoo
(312) 742-2000

Late October
Boo at the Zoo
Brookfield Zoo
(708) 485-0263

NOVEMBER
Late November
Magnificent Mile Lights Festival
N. Michigan Ave.
(312) 409-5560

Late November
Field's Jingle Elf Parade
State St.
(312) 744-3370

Late November
City of Chicago Tree Lighting
Ceremony
Daley Plaza
(312) 744-3370

**Late November to late
December**
Holiday Magic
Brookfield Zoo
(708) 485-0263

**Late November to late
December**
ZooLights Festival
Lincoln Park Zoo
(312) 742-2000

**Late November to early
January**
Celebration of Lights
Garfield Park Conservatory
(312) 746-5100

DECEMBER
Early December
Julmarknad
Swedish American Museum
Center
(773) 728-8111

Early December
Latino Book & Family Festival
McCormick Place
(312) 255-9206

Late December
New Year's Eve S.A.F.E. (Safe,
alcohol-free family events)
Various locations around
Chicago
(312) 747-2606

INDEX